SpringerWien NewYork

CONSEQUENCE BOOK SERIES ON FRESH ARCHITECTURE VOL. 2

HERAUSGEGEBEN VON / EDITED BY
iCP - INSTITUTE FOR CULTURAL POLICY

MARCOSANDMARJAN

INTERFACES / INTRAFACES

Springer Wien New York

iCP – Institute for Cultural Policy

Leitung / Direction:
Patrick Ehrhardt
Wolfgang Fiel

www.i-c-p.org

© 2005 Springer-Verlag/Wien
Printed in Austria
SpringerWienNewYork is a part of
Springer Science+Business Media
springeronline.com

Umschlagbilder Cover illustrations:
© 2005 marcosandmarjan
Layout:
Andreas Berlinger; London / BARBARA SAYS... ; Lisbon
Druck Printing: Holzhausen Druck & Medien GmbH
1140 Wien, Österreich

Gedruckt auf säurefreiem, chlorfrei gebleichtem Papier - TCF
Printed on acid-free and chlorine-free bleached paper
SPIN: 11404057

Mit zahlreichen (großteils farbigen) Abbildungen
With numerous (mainly coloured) illustrations

Bibliografische Informationen Der Deutschen Bibliothek
Die Deutsche Bibliothek verzeichnet diese Publikation in der
Deutschen Nationalbibliografie; detaillierte bibliografische
Daten sind im Internet über <http://dnb.ddb.de> abrufbar.

ISBN-10 3-211-25232-0 SpringerWienNewYork
ISBN-13 978-3-211-25232-1 SpringerWienNewYork

Consequence: Rendering the boundaries

`Is urban architecture in the process of becoming a technology just as outdated as extensive farming? Will architectonics become nothing more than a decadent form of dominating the earth, with consequences analogous to the unbridled exploitation of raw materials? Hasn't the decline in the number of cities also become the symbol of industrial decline and forced unemployment, the symbol of scientific materialism's failure? (...) The crisis of modernity's grand narratives, about which Lyotard speaks, betrays the presence of new technology, with the emphasis being placed, from now on, on the „means" and not on the „ends"´ (Virilio 1999).

In Anknüpfung an obiges Zitat von Paul Virilio gehen wir von der These aus, dass das Berufsbild der ArchitektIn einem grundsätzlichen poststrukturalistischen Wandel unterliegt. Mit der Immersion der digitalen Medien und elektronischen Apparate muss die Definition des architektonischen Raums einer grundsätzlichen und zeitgemäßen Revision unterzogen werden. Während das psychische Modell des modernistischen Raumparadigmas mit der Echtzeiterfahrung im physischen Realraum noch kongruent war und durch die Regeln der klassischen Perspektive hinreichend beschrieben werden konnte, führt die rhizomatische Organisation der Datennetzwerke an den Schnittstellen global verteilter Userterminals zum Verlust der Wahrnehmung räumlicher Tiefe zugunsten einer kinematografischen Zeittiefe. Die Ästhetik stabiler Bilder wird durch die Ästhetik des beschleunigten Verschwindens labiler Bilder ersetzt. Räumliche Exploration erfolgt nunmehr weltumspannend an jedem beliebigen Ort, während Simultanität in elastischen Zeitintervallen erfolgt und durch die „Trägheit des Auges" bestimmt wird.

Das heisst aber auch, dass wir einen Paradigmenwechsel von der Repräsentation zur Interpretation vollziehen, der eng mit der Frage nach der Konstituierung brauchbarer Schnittstellen verbunden ist. Die von Virilio angesprochene Verlagerung von der Zielfunktion (ends) zur Wahl der Mittel (means) im Rahmen einer prozesshaften Kultur des Ereignisses entspricht gleichzeitig einer Verschiebung von der Metaebene eines dialektischen Theoriebegriffs zur mikropolitischen Praxis improvisatorischen Handelns.

Mit der Auswahl der im Rahmen der Ausstellungsreihe „consequence" präsentierten ArchitektInnen soll die gängige Praxis gegenwärtiger Architekturproduktion hinterfragt werden. Sie verkörpern auf exemplarische Weise die vielfältigen Ausdrucksformen im Zuge der skizzierten Neudefinition des Berufsbilds. Die jeweiligen Tätigkeitsfelder sind durch die systematische Entwicklung partikularer Forschungsschwerpunkte gekennzeichnet, einer Art mikropolitischer und methodischer Praxis an den Rändern der eigenen Profession sowie im transdisziplinären Crossover unterschiedlicher Disziplinen. Die Arbeitsweisen haben einen Hang zum Technologischen, sind narrativ, performativ, spekulativästhetisch und verfügen über ein Problembewusstsein, das auf einer konzeptuellen Ebene verankert ist oder am spezifischen Kontext festgemacht werden kann. Mit der Auswahl soll auf eine Generation aufmerksam gemacht werden, die mit ihren Arbeiten neue diskursive Räume erschließt.

Wolfgang Fiel, Hamburg, Juni 2005

Virilio, P 1999, `The overexposed city´, in Druckrey, T. & Ars Electronica (eds.), Facing The Future, MIT Press, Cambridge, pp. 276-283.

Editorial Notice

Consequence: Rendering the boundaries

`Is urban architecture in the process of becoming a technology just as outdated as extensive farming? Will architectonics become nothing more than a decadent form of dominating the earth, with consequences analogous to the unbridled exploitation of raw materials? Hasn't the decline in the number of cities also become the symbol of industrial decline and forced unemployment, the symbol of scientific materialism's failure? (...) The crisis of modernity's grand narratives, about which Lyotard speaks, betrays the presence of new technology, with the emphasis being placed, from now on, on the „means" and not on the „ends"´ (Virilio 1999).

Following up to the statement from Paul Virilio, the claim is set out, that the profession of the architect currently undergoes a significant post-structuralist change. With the immersion of digital media and electronic apparatus the definition of physical space and its perception has to be fundamentally revised. Whilst the psychological imprint of the modernistic dimension of space was specified by significant „time distances" in relation to physical obstacles, represented by the rules of perspective, the rhizomatic nature of electronic networks - accessable via the interfaces of globally distributed userterminals – has subsequently led to the loss of spatial depth in exchange for the cinematic depth of time. The believe in the enduring objectives of dualistic determinism has been succeeded by an aesthetic of the accelerated disappearance of transient images. The exhaustion of temporal distance creates a telescoping of any localization, at any position and any time, for it simultaneity is measured in elastic time-intervalls equivalent to the retinal persistance - the after image.

Likewise we face a paradigmatic change from the era of representation to one of interpretation which is closely bound to the need of creating operable interfaces. In the light of the turn from the „ends" to the „means" as aforementioned, a process-oriented culture of events would cause an improvisational turn from the meta-level of the dialectic theory-notion toward a micropolitical practice.

With the choice of architects within the scope of „consequence", well established modernistic modes of architectural representation are challenged. All of these architects embody a wide range of formal expression, as a result of their unique endeavour in research and architectonic practice alike. Their particular fields of activity are characterized by a tentative policy in exploring and augmenting the boundaries of the profession as well as to foster a prolific interchange with other disciplines. The modes of operation are technological, often do follow narratives, are performative, speculative in their account for novel aesthetics and demonstrate a sensible awareness for current local phenomena and global developments, which can be tied to a specific context or are expressed on a conceptual level. With the choice for fresh accounts from a new generation of experimental architects, we aim to launch new territories of discourse.

Wolfgang Fiel, Hamburg, June 2005

Virilio, P. 1999, `The overexposed city´, in Druckrey, T. & Ars Electronica (eds.), Facing The Future, MIT Press, Cambridge, pp. 276-283.

Über / About iCP

Das `Institute for Cultural Policy´, wurde 2004 als unabhängige und interdisziplinäre Forschungseinrichtung in Hamburg/Deutschland gegründet. Das iCP bietet die Infrastruktur und ist diskursive Plattform für die Förderung und Weiterentwicklung des Austausches zwischen Architektur, Kunst, Wissenschaft und Industrie.

The `Institute for Cultural Policy´, was founded in 2004 as an independent and cross-disciplinary research institution in Hamburg/Germany. The iCP provides the infrastructure and is a platform for discourse fostering a prolific exchange between architecture, art, science and industry.

Danksagung / Acknowledgements

Die Herausgeber bedanken sich bei allen, die am Zustandekommen des Projekts beteiligt waren, im Speziellen Alexandra Berlinger, Andreas Berlinger, Amelie Graalfs, David Marold, Beatrice Peini Gysen-Hsieh sowie Marcos Cruz und Marjan Colletti für die ausgezeichnete Zusammenarbeit.

● 3

MARCOSANDMARJAN IN HAMBURG
by <u>Peter Cook</u> · London 2005

The clue to this work surely lies in its paradoxes of its
aspirations: there is the search for "poetic automatism" or
"symbolic bliss, which can exclude the confrontation with the
real" among the many that intrigue one in Marjan Colletti's
essay 'Mimetic Intrafaces'. Yet simultaneously, Marcos Cruz,
under the banner of 'Inhabitable Interfaces' can delight in the
"unprecedented ornamental richness of sensuous attraction
...of the Baroque", or in voyeurism.

In some seven years' observation of these two architects I
must, (as usual), refuse to take anything at face value. Just
as they seemed to when studiously avoiding each other whilst
in the same postgraduate class, yet realising their affinities
a year or two later. Studied disinterest is an observable characteristic of clever young architects, but few have the guts to
move past that and realise that creativity is a more precious
thing than positioning. So too is the kaleidoscopic culture
that begat them: which might puzzle or enfeeble weaker
minds, but seems only to create a resource upon which their
increasingly mature design work is bedded.

If Marcos displays the logic and proceduralism of the German
side of his background it serves to order (and actually make
accessible) the edgier and more flamboyant tastes of the Portuguese side. For Marjan the South Tyrolean condition must be
pocketed differently and it is significant that he, though communicating with Marcos in German, was exposed not to German culture <u>per-se</u> but to its debased (or rather, re-invented)

form in Austria. From Innsbruck, you could always return through the mountain pass to the side where the intensity of it all might be relieved by a more languid Italian infiltration. And they have remained in London. That now not-very-English city whose greatest asset is its coagulation of flight-paths and similarly scrambled conversations. Where the tradition of speculation is stronger than the Franco-American traditions of reference and verification. So far they seem to have remained in control of these forces and have pursued so many design projects whilst simultaneously teaching and writing dissertations.

At face value, the work reflects these pressures, curiously, more so in a catalogue or book than on the wall. It has to explain, and these guys are good at explaining and dissertations force you to do this (with all those academically mandatory but oh-so-tiresome references), whereas a scheme is a scheme. It is stuff. Sure, the observer can sniff out the influences, but in a design project you don't _have_ to verify, you don't _have_ to be consistent, you don't _have_ to underline. In space the head can wander and Marjan's 'symbolic bliss' can occur without a feeling of intellectual guilt.

So if I look at a modest series of projects, the 'Nurbsters', they summarise the situation very well. First of all its title: Marjan is brilliant at setting-up the creative title: the title that pulls the projects along whilst slightly mystifying the onlooker. So out of 'Besking' and 'Bartsters' come these contraptions. Incorporating the bliss of the digital cutter, the ease of MDF, the opportunity to do a piece of design that will focus and enhance the otherwise commonplace moment of student shows, the reiteration of the theme of non-uniform rational B-splines, hence: NURBS. It creates an architecture of Marcos' favourite occupied wall. They are slinky, sexy, but cheap!

I have tremendous respect for such projects and the predicament they represent. For several of Marcos and Marjan's contemporaries would perhaps have developed a series of intellectual themes and confined them to the dissertation or to

some seminar discussions. They might make elegant five-finger exercises on the computer (or with a deftly held pencil), whereby the possibility of three-dimensional bliss is implied. Other, hairier individuals might expend their energies on building a constructional toy, full of natty joints and – "oh my goodness– it all folds up into the back of a VW!"
– But no. Marcos and Marjan used the opportunity to continue exercising those most important ingredients: their collective talent, the Moment and the need to continually push and pull away at their ideas. So the really interesting aspect of this series is that it extends, illuminates and exercises their other projects, reminding us that these guys are driven and are going somewhere. And they are made. As the series develops it manages to delve and twist; becoming proto-architecture, which is something different from model-making in that you can really get above, below, alongside and within. You can enjoy sensuous attraction – even of MDF, no, certainly of MDF!

So one approaches the project for the Lisbon Book fair auditorium and cafeteria with less surprise at its apparent maturity and intrigue. Sure, it is faceted rather than moulded – but at this pace of creativity the moulded building will surely come – but it is swung out into space, folded and they call it a lizard. It is unafraid of its componentry and deals with the use of scaffolding without the pedantry or awe of the aforementioned 'hairy' architects. Another important step in the joy of stuff (empowered – so that's OK theoretically – by the magic of computer modelling and cutting).

I cannot observe their work without constantly noting their role as teachers and observers of talent. Volcker Giencke once described his memories of Marjan as his nuttiest student in Innsbruck and (it was late at night), as the reminiscences became more graphic, the table in Vienna's Salzamt weaved its way across the floor. By contrast (but not really), Marcos became one of the first graduate students at the Bartlett to already be a more articulate and informed critic than most of his teachers – and still to like stuff and materiality and the byways of stuff rather than the down-the-line consistencies. Developing the competition stage of the Graz Kunsthaus, it was Marcos' disgustingly floppy tube experiments that egged us on to breed the alien. It was his project for trapped bodies in skins that remains in the mind as an alternative interpretation than the predictable wafts and waves of so much digitalised surfboarding.

One is aware of this in projects such as the Tomihiro 'Garden of Vessels' which resolves the garden of tubes into a cleverly succinct plan whereby the contribution of the circular geometry is not allowed to coarsen the total body. The diagrams in which Marcos compares various buildings with inhabitable interfaces, including their own with a series of more-or-less heroic examples, serves to toughen the general approach. Bernard Tschumi is a past master at this, whereby the logic of plan and section analysis becomes a necessary adjunct to the poetics of automatism or the delight in the ornamental richness of sensual attraction.

They become increasingly able to push and pull and weave around space, so the Lofting House can enjoy its directional wraps and writhing staircases, the proposal for the Azores International Fair can prepare (almost) to flap its extraordinary wings whilst still revealing - for the connoisseur - a very juicy and yet urbane plan. Yes, these guys really come out of architecture: take a look at some of those plans again, for the sheer sophistication of the organisation of the Xiyuan Entertainment Complex recalls that of the first larger projects of Morphosis. And look what has happened to them! The similarity is not in terms of the mannerisms or stylisation or even in approach to then direction of the computer - but in really understanding the power and hierarchies of parts, the opportunities for delving and tucking and parts that live within other parts. As the roofs sweep over, they are potentially filled with magic.

Wonderfully rich and effusive stuff, when they have finally put away their dissertations, we can stand back and watch them really fly and watch their more timid (or lazier) contemporaries try to explain it all away.

MIMETIC INTRAFACES
by <u>Marjan Colletti</u>

<u>Definition//Geometry</u>

Within a discourse on digital architecture, it is important to distinguish between the concepts of <u>inter</u>face—in most general terms described as the <u>boundary</u> between two disparate systems—and <u>intra</u>face—here described as a <u>homologous framework</u> <u>bounded</u> inside a controlled feedback system. On the contrary to dissociated and symmetric (both sides are equal, but different and separated), or direct and analogous (interface is similar in function but not in structure and evolutionary origin to both sides) human-machine environments, intrafaces act in a homologous manner: similarities exist in the whole system's structure and evolutionary origin, though not necessarily in its function. Under these circumstances, rather than <u>operating</u> in one direction as screen, monitor, or display, the intraface <u>performs</u> screening, monitoring, or displaying within a controlled feedback system.

Whereby earlier research undertaken in the discipline of Human-Computer Interactions (HCI) endeavoured to abbreviate the distance between user and interface, the typological turn of interfaces into intrafaces implies a geometric transition from line to <u>convoluted field</u>. A convoluted field resembles Greg Lynn's depiction of an 'intricate network', where detail is "everywhere, ubiquitously distributed and continuously variegated in collaboration with formal and spatial effects. ... Intricacy occurs where macro- and micro-scales of components are interwoven and intertwined."[1] Based on the concept of intricacy, Lynn suggests a system of fusion,

(cont. p. 26)

RENDER//SHADE//WIREFRAMES

The so-called 'Zero Space Theory' describes a universe where every point is occupied twice by the same field existing in different phases, described by Mark Messer as the condensed 'matter state', and the free 'space fabric' state.[1] Similarly, every volumetric digital entity entails a twofold presence, which may be described in the first stance as a 'fabric' interwoven by defining curves, in the second stance as an 'image' portrayed by defining pixels. The first state of a digitally created entity, as fabric defined by interwoven curves, may be considered its quantitative condition within the digital space of three-dimensional software packages. The second, condensed matter state as portrayed by defining pixels and embodied by rendered images, may be depicted as the digital entity's qualitative conditions. All 3D CAD software packages allow different ways of displaying digital space, the most common being: in wireframe, shaded, rendered (OpenGL, Phong, etc.), and hidden mode. On-screen shaded or rendered views simplify and approximate existing interactions and relationships between geometries and entities, lights and colours, materials and textures, transparencies and shadows. Rendered pixel graphics of vector based drawings on the other hand calculate and depict quantitative and qualitative data with

NEW GODET CLUB
MARCOSANDMARJAN • 2003

COMPETITION PROPOSAL FOR THE NEW TOMIHIRO
MUSEUM • MARCOSANDMARJAN • 2002

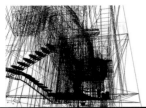

detail. Akin to some artists' work or to '
photography, renderings present themselves as two-dimensional projections
of three-dimensional spatial properties
and volumetric entities of digital space,
and as snapshots of spatial-temporal
defined circumstances. As in a photo-
graphic process, volumes, lights, transparencies, etc. are captured through
a device and developed on a picture
frame—in photography on the negative
film (or directly to photosensitive paper
as in Polaroid), and in renderings on the
screen (or directly to file).

- -

[1] Mark Messer, A 'Zero Space' Theory.

'aggregation', and 'assemblage' where diverse elements are
linked into a continuous, whole composition. Nonetheless, a
convoluted field, far more than a complex system, is capable
of developing beyond the stochastic function of intricacy into
a structure that allows multiple or even infinite linkages and
communications patterns independently from the amount of
components, even tolerating the probability of any module to
resemble zero.

Likewise, convoluted fields can be infinite, for they
could be null at the same time; that is, they can express
a phenomenological conception of existence (1), yet
simultaneously an ontological notion of virtuality (0). In
Zero is 'Infinite' not Empty, James N. Rose[2] explains how
the symbol 0 (zero) was introduced to create a space for
the potential for positive numbers to exist, gaining its own
identity and existence as placeholder for potential. In the
1960s and '70s Rose defined it as a form of behaviour space,
and later in the mid 1990s he wrote that any "existential
system to be must exist in an extended environment … which
shares some factor of compatibility." Andre Linde then
went on to explicate the possibility of different universes in
'interactable region' described by him as 'existence space'.

- -

[1] Greg Lynn, Intricacy, catalogue to the exhibition ‚Intricacy', guest curated by G. Lynn at the
Institute of Contemporary Art, University of Philadelphia, 18.01 - 06.04.2003.
[2] James N. Rose, Zero is 'Infinite' not Empty, Bulletin #11, April 16, 1998, http://www.
ceptualinstitute.com

Tasks//Function

In the Editorial Notice to this book, Wolfgang Fiel foresees "a
paradigmatic change from the era of representation to one of
interpretation which is closely bound to the need of creating
operable interfaces." In fact, against the assumptions
that computer aided architecture serves mere commercial
illustrative objectives, the task of a digital mimetic intraface
does not convey the notion of a (Platonic) form of imitation
and simulation, but delineates a (Freudian) process of blissful
direct creative engagement with things, objects, and forms.
Whilst interface expresses and mediates different sets of
goals on and between its system and human side, intraface

exists and acts amid complex domains, or fields, engaging in an inclusive, interpretative process of the surrounding environment: <u>digital mimesis</u>.

Distinct aspects of 'directness'[3] have already been highlighted by the discipline of HCI, providing a characterisation of interfaces in relationship to aspects of 'distance'—between the user's thoughts and the physical needs of system and user—and 'direct engagement'—the user's sensation of direct action on the system's objects and tasks.[4] As Brenda Laurel argues in <u>Computers as Theatre</u>, direct engagement emphasises emotional as well as cognitive values, and introduces artistic and aesthetic considerations into the discipline's functional agenda, leading her to formulate human-computer interaction as 'designed experience", in which '<u>pleasure</u> and <u>engagement</u>' are possible.[5]

Beyond models of directness, intrafaces used for architectural design purposes ought to challenge the trade's aim at hyperrealism and parametric calculation, allowing pleasure, fantasy and bliss to enlarge the aesthetic, tectonic and topological vocabulary of digital space. In such a context, intraface as John Frazer's "electronic muse"[6] may be capable of Karl S. Chu's "gnostic quest for fulfillment"[7].

In a Heideggerian understanding the computer brings forth and exposes; yet whereby rather than technologically revealing the real as standing-reserve, it bestows man with new ways of expressing the Mystérique. Therefore, on a conceptual level, the intraface must have shaken off its dust of self-organising, representational, abstract Turing machine (forerunner to later developments of binary computers), and should being perceived as capable of producing <u>poetic automatism</u>; it is poetic since it produces Mollinian poetic images[8]—as the convergence of expression and intuition—and it expresses automatism for its Baudrillardian status of synthesising "absolute singularity" with "infinite seriality".[9] Poetic automatism does not aspire at the mechanisation of the body or the eye, but at the amalgamation and convergence

CONTROL POINTS//SPLINEAR FABRIC
NURBS entities are defined by control points that can be located outside the physical (albeit digital) boundaries of the object itself. The NURBS surface, built up by a series of curves defining its geometry, is only visible as volumetric entity when shaded or rendered. Borrowing from mathematician Andre Linde's and Lynn's terminology, it may be stated that NURBS entities are 'interactable' elements in the bounds of the digital 'existence' realm are possible because of their 'flexible topological' expressions within spline-controlled rather than point-controlled systems. In this context pixel-graphics must adhere to point-controlled systems, and are therefore inflexible in dynamic topological terms. Thus argues Lynn that "dynamic modelling systems are based on the interaction of multiple parameter statements calculated sequentially rather than in an instant."[2] This notion of sequence invokes the spline and the existence of intrinsic control (and feedback) points as an adequate geometrical element in order to describe possible behavioural spaces within the splinear fabric of threedimensional convoluted field.

- -
[2] Greg Lynn, <u>Animate Form</u>, Princeton Architectural Press, New York, 1999, p. 25.

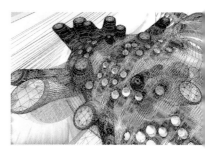

COMPETITION PROPOSAL FOR THE NEW
TOMIHIRO MUSEUM · MARCOSANDMARJAN · 2002

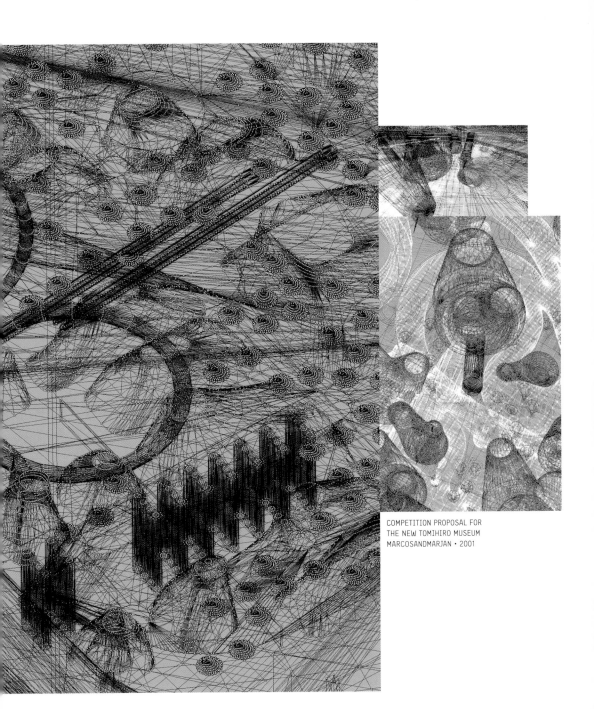

COMPETITION PROPOSAL FOR
THE NEW TOMIHIRO MUSEUM
MARCOSANDMARJAN · 2001

Nurbster I . Installation for Unit 20

Bartfest 04 - Slade School of Art UCL, London UK [July 2004]
Young British Architecture - Fragnera Gallery, Prague Czech Republic [Oct.-Dec. 2004]

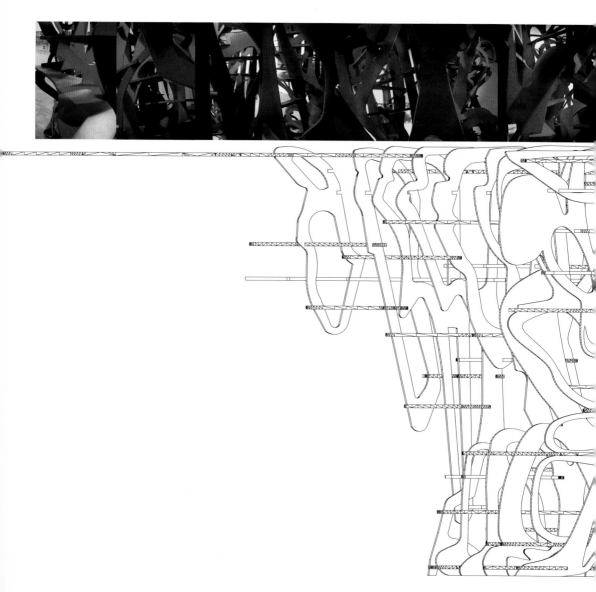

Team » Design: marcosandmarjan with Unit 20 › Assembling: Students of Unit 20 › Manufacturing: Zone Creations › Sponsor: The Great Britain Sasakawa Foundation

- -

The NURBSTER features two kinds of components that are cut by CAD-operated machines out of standard-sized MDF boards: enclosed vertical loops and singular horizontal stripes. The separate pieces are assembled to form a skeleton-like wall for the Unit 20 End of Year Show at the Bartfest 2004 integrating student projects developed in Japan. The NURBSTER adapts traditional Japanese wooden construction techniques of cut-joint fittings without additional fixings for quick assembly and disassembly.

A series of layered sections create a complex volume of NURBS (non-uniform rational B-splines), expressed through curvilinear and arabesque geometries that blur the boundaries between the horizontal and vertical frames. Slaloming back and forth, as well as up and down, switching viewpoint between the more corporeal/volumetric and the more transparent/permeable sides, the eye tends to scan the NURBSTER obliquely. Within the wall space, light renders gradients all along the edges and the planar surfaces; an idea tested in the colouration of early cutting-paths drawings.

NURBSTER I IN EXHIBITION AT THE
SLADE SCHOOL OF ART IN LONDON

Nurbster II . Exhibition Table

Metaflux – Architecture Biennial, Corderie dell'Arsenale, Venice Italy [12.09.04-07.11.04]
Metaflux – Cordoaria Nacional, Lisbon Portugal [11.12.04-30.01.05]
Metaflux – Fundação Tomie Ohtake, São Paulo Brasil [17.05.05-10.07.05]

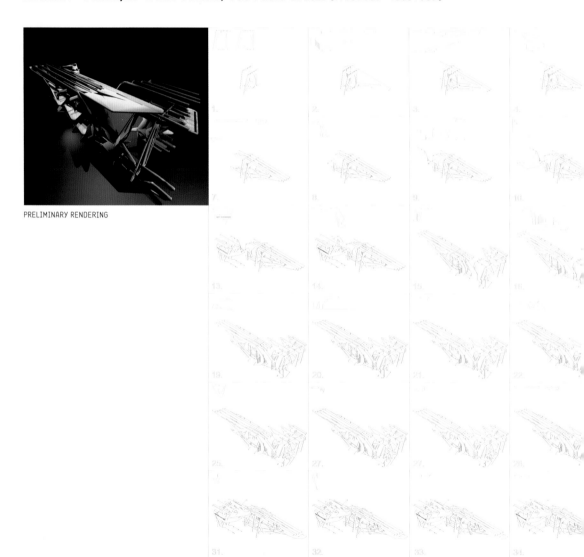

PRELIMINARY RENDERING

CONSTRUCTION MANUAL

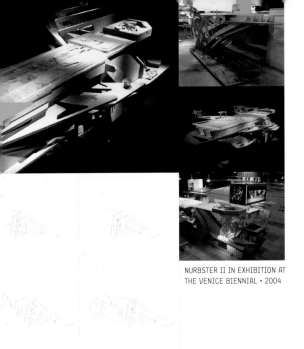

NURBSTER II IN EXHIBITION AT
THE VENICE BIENNIAL · 2004

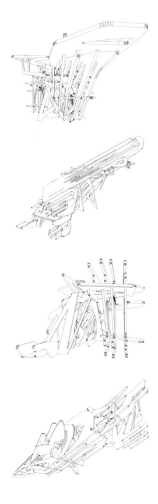

Team » Design: marcosandmarjan › Collaborators: Nat Keast, Samuel White, Mark Andrews › Manufacturing: Zone Creations

- -

The NURBSTER II consists of a table for exhibition purposes that features a series of models and objects by marcosandmarjan at the Metaflux exhibition during the Venice Biennale 2004. Created through CAD/CAM processes, it follows previous experiments for Unit 20 exhibitions at the Bartlett School of Architecture, UCL. Its ornamental character expresses deliberate design eccentricities within the precision and material efficiency of the CAD-operated process. It adapts traditional oriental wooden construction techniques of cut-joint fittings without additional fixings for quick assembly and disassembly.

Nurbster III - Bartsters

Installation for the exhibition Young British Architecture
New Designs from the Bartlett School of Architecture, UCL
at the Jaroslava Fragnera Gallery, Prague Czech Republic, 2004 [28.10.04-12.12.04]

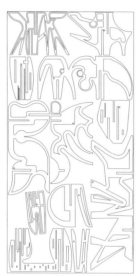

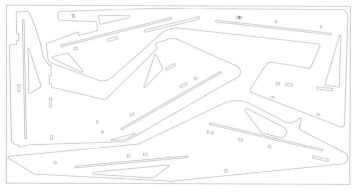
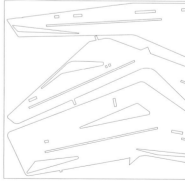

PRELIMINARY RENDERING OF
ALUMINIUM BOARDS

GENERAL VIEW OF EXHIBITION

NURBSTER III - DETAIL

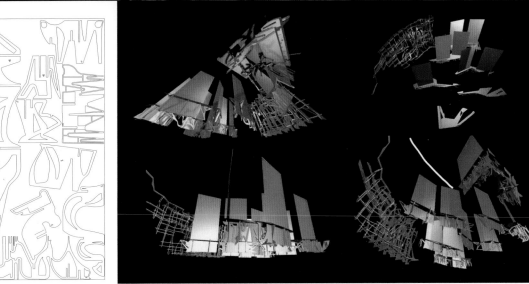

PLYWOOD BOARDS PREPARED
FOR WATER JETTING

ALUMINIUM BOARDS PREPARED
FOR LASER CUTTING

Client » British Council Czech Republic
Team » Design: Marjan Colletti › Collaborators: Alex Kirkwood, Frank Gilks,
Nat Keast › Assembling: Mark Exon › Manufacturing: Control Waterjet Cutting

- -

The main exhibition design features six (plus one, the Nurbster I) laser-cut
aluminium and water-jetted plywood display islands, presenting student work
from the Bartlett School of Architecture, UCL London. Due to the work's tantalis-
ing and teasing nature, the 'Bartsters' resemble hybrids between sailing-boats
and insects, pleasingly cruising, and viciously creeping, into the imagination
of both the students and architects visiting the exhibition.

This construction adapts traditional Chinese timber construction techniques of
cut-joint fittings without additional fixings for quick assembly and disassembly.

Nurbster IV - Splinewall

Feng Chia & Bartlett

Digital Architecture Workshop, Taichung Taiwan, 2005-08-18

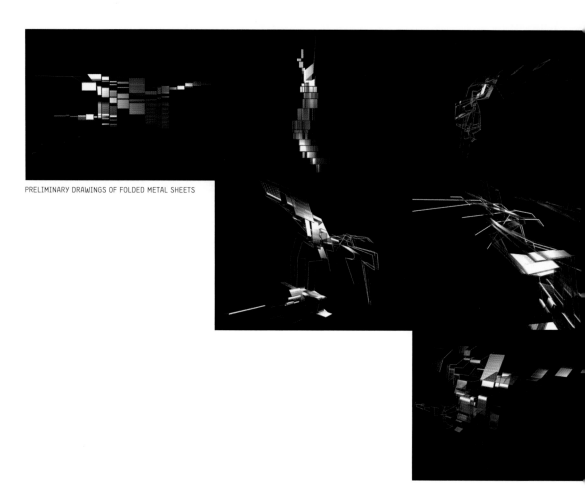

PRELIMINARY DRAWINGS OF FOLDED METAL SHEETS

PRELIMINARY RENDERING OF SPLINEWALL

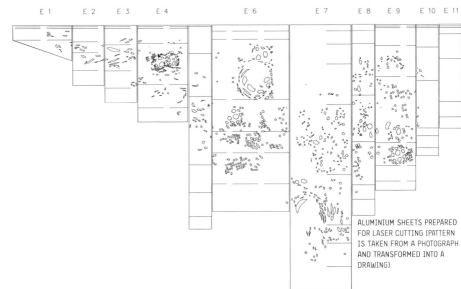

E 1   E 2   E 3   E 4   E 6   E 7   E 8   E 9   E 10 E 11

ALUMINIUM SHEETS PREPARED
FOR LASER CUTTING (PATTERN
IS TAKEN FROM A PHOTOGRAPH
AND TRANSFORMED INTO A
DRAWING)

20 ●

SPLINEWALL IN EXHIBITION AT FENG CHIA UNIVERSITY

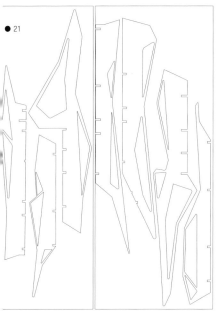

ALUMINIUM SHEETS
(BILLBOARD AND ROOF STRIPES)
PREPARED FOR LASER CUTTING

Team » Design / Tutors: marcosandmarjan › Workshop Organizers: Simon Shu, Beatrice Hsien, (Trudi Ko) › Students: Tze-Chun Wei (Jim), Wen-Ting Chang (Wendy), Chi-Chih Mao (Chi Chi), Po-Chuan Chen (Paul), Fang-Wei Tsao, Li-Wu Wang (Wu), Hsueh-Chan Yang (Akira), Ping-Hsun Li (Bob), Chun Wan, Ping-Chen Liu (Benson), Chih-Chien Liao (Ray), Chun-Hung Chen, Meng-Hung Cheng (Sam), Tsung-Yu Tsai, Tung-Chieh Su (Victor), Shu-Min Fu (Sumi), Pin-Chi Yu (Erik), Yao-Hui Huang (Grace), Chen-An Pan (Pan), Chien-Min Chen (Steven), Kuo-Pang Hsiao (Shawn), Ke-Hsiu Wu (Louis), Wei-Ti Huang (Jason), Yu Hsuan Huang (Fred), Chun-Teng Li (Ivy), Tze Hau Chen (Pika Chen) › Laser Cutting: Chun-Sheng Industry Limited Company, Taichung Taiwan

- -

The Splinewall installation was created during the "Digital Architecture Design Unit and Workshop Exhibition" hold by Feng Chia University. 26 selected architecture students under the direction of marcosandmarjan took 9 days to develop the construction.

One group starts by questioning traditional wall concepts and the interaction between usersand the architectural skin. Simultaneously, another group observes animal features and translates them into possible digital constructs. Their intuitive personal responses are then transferred into abstract patterns, and later materialised in a collective architectural piece by using 3D software. This construction adapts traditional Chinese timber construction techniques of cut-joint fittings without additional fixings for quick assembly and disassembly. The boards are laser cut in a factory outside the university and later assembled in the final exhibition space.

This Splinewall is 6 metres long and 3 metres high, consisting out of an interior and an exterior wall. The exterior wall and the roof is made out of metal sheets. The interior wall is constructed out of wood and hosts a seating facility for animation projections on an incorporated digital screen.

This construction adapts traditional Chinese wooden construction techniques of cut-joint fittings without additional fixings for quick assembly and disassembly

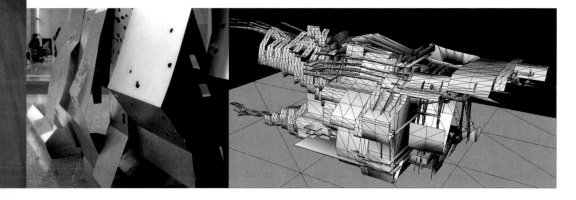

Nurbster V – FLL Folies

Proposal for a Folie with incorporated sitting facilities
at the 75th Lisbon Book Fair 2005, Lisbon Portugal, 2005

PRELIMINARY RENDERINGS
LOFTING OF EXTERNAL VOLUME

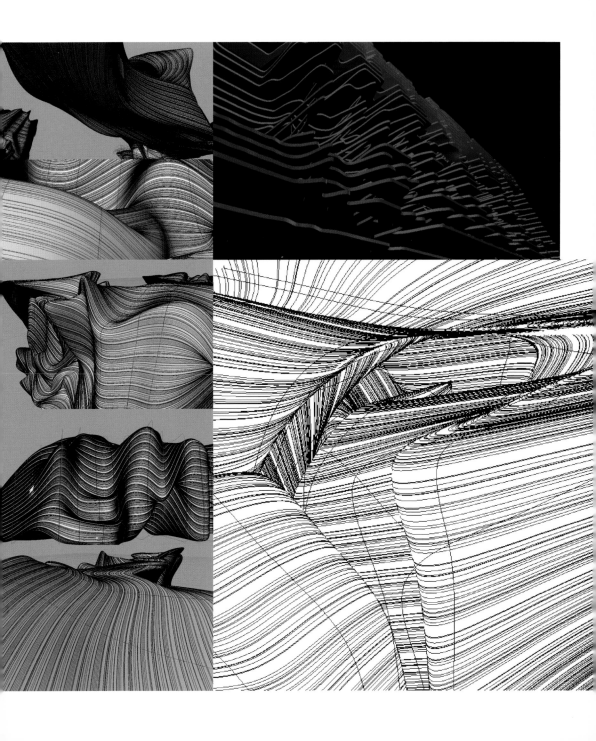

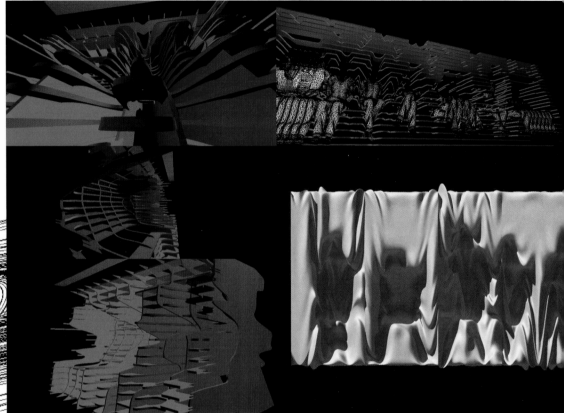

Client » Câmara Municipal de Lisboa, EGEAC
Team » Design: marcosandmarjan › Collaborators: João Albuquerque, Shui Liu,
Marco Sacchi › Associate Architects: Guedes & Viinikainen › Associate Engineer:
Francisco Bernardo - A400 › Graphic Design: Barbara Says...
› Laser Cutting: Lasindústria › Construction: Contubos
Construction cost: 500.000.00 Euros › Programme: General layout of Book Fair,
Cafeteria, Auditorium, Outside Esplanade, Information Pavilion
Total construction area: 1000m²

- -

The 75th Lisbon Book Fair is characterised by a variety of spaces and atmospheres to be discovered while walking along the Boulevards on both sides of
the Parque Eduardo VII. Against the traditional layout of stands and pavilions
aligned in parallel rows, this proposal's organisation positions the stands
around several open areas in order to form small squares with a strong urban
feeling. These spaces are differentiated by their spatial arrangement and

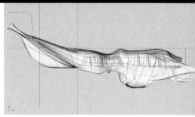

BODY ANATOMIES SEEN FROM BEHIND

IN-WALL SITTING
ERGONOMIC STUDIES OF BODIES WITHIN
THE NURBSTER CONSTRUCTION

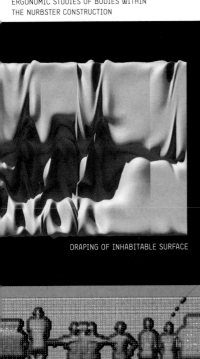

DRAPING OF INHABITABLE SURFACE

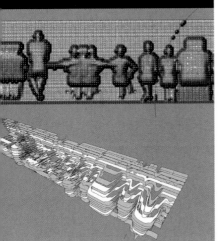

colour, being simultaneously resting spaces, and areas where specific activities for the publishers can take place.

The access to fair is permitted from different sides and punctuated by main public pavilions. But it is on the north side that the most iconographic infrastructures are implanted: the information pavilion on the top of the eastern boulevard, and the cafeteria and auditorium on the top of the western boulevard; the last one being a structure that is projected from the street level down to the middle of the park.

The architecture project that accompanies the fair integrates a 1000m2 construction of three independent structures: an auditorium for a minimum of 150 people, a self-service cafeteria with an exterior esplanade for 70 people and an information pavilion. Differently form other years, the proposal links the auditorium and the cafeteria through a large staircase, which allows the seating area of the auditorium to be extended to the outside. This solution of a created amphitheatre permits the users of the cafeteria to watch the cultural activities inside the auditorium, while appreciating the views over the city from the outside or through the large window opening behind the stage. This auditorium can host not just the cultural events linked to the book fair, as well as have concerts or theatre performances that can be enjoyed from the outside when the sliding doors are opened during the warm summer nights. It later became re-entitled as 'Sky Lounge' and reutilised as a high level club for special events in the park during the following summer months.

The sculptural expression of the building publishes the inner events through its strong visual impact in the surrounding landscape: the bar announces the fair through a cantilever, which is projected over the pavement of the street; the auditorium is extended down into the green area right into the middle of the park. It is visible from a great distance, such as the Avenida da Liberdade or even from the S. Jorge castle. The volume of the auditorium is characterised through a sequence of inclined red surfaces, into which the logo of the fair is laser cut. This volume is central to the whole fair and accessible from three sides, with various perspectival conditions, as if it were three distinct buildings.

The structure is nick named 'lizard' because of the way in which it lies in the topography of the park (original project by architect Keil do Amaral during the years of the Portuguese dictatorship) and how it overviews the city. The diagonal disposition of the structure and its strong horizontality reinforces the wish to break the symmetry of the park and stands in contrast to the vertical presence of the pre-exiting columns, nevertheless incorporating them into the overall design. Due to the temporary nature of the building and the speed of its construction (4 weeks), as well as the impossibility to ground it with foundations, the construction was quickly assembled with a scaffolding structure surrounded by an exterior mdf cladding, both of which to be reutilised.

The three-dimensional complexity of the building topography forced the process to be determined by intensive 3D computer modelling, afterwards controlled by 2D drawings illustrating a large series of sequential sections and plans.

of the body with the world of imagination. Its production is driven by poetry rather than mechanistic, by poiesis rather than techné. Here as in a Carlo Mollino, technology does not aim at the production of poetry, but simply as bringing at man's disposal new pretexts and ways of expression. Also, based on Jean Baudrillard's conception of automatism going further than animism for its strive for 'supra-functionality of human consciousness'[10], poetic automatism never minds performing formal, fantasy operations, which do not answer real practical collective needs and operate in the imaginary realm rather than in the real.

As brought forth by Žižek in <u>From Virtual Reality to the Virtualisation of Reality</u>, fantasy in Lacanian terms is the ultimate support of reality; reality, that performs as background for 'symbolic bliss', which can exclude the confrontation with the Real and lets reality stabilise itself.[11] As pointed out by Lacan, the computer can be regarded as the archetypical case for 'symbolic bliss'[12] if one conceives it as a 'thinking machine' (<u>machine à penser</u>) inscribing itself into our symbolic universe, and thus acting as an 'evocatory object'[13]: an objects which, beyond its technical instrumental function, in Žižek's words, 'raises a whole series of basic questions about the specificity of human thought, about the difference between animate and inanimate, etc.'[14] Although the distance between the virtual and the actual realm has concerned architects for decades, the frustration with virtuality's aloofness, detachment and disembodiment can be overcome, if the computer is understood as intraface capable of inventing realities and entities close to the heart's desire, which are adopted into our everyday cognition, enhancing reality with many layers of fiction and emotional narrative.

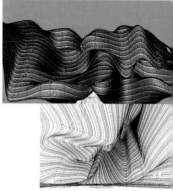

LOFTING OF NURBSTER STRUCTURE
FLL FOLIES
MARCOSANDMARJAN · 2005

- -

[3] Donald A. Norman, 'Cognitive Engineering', pp. 31-61, in <u>User Centered System Design – New Perspectives on Human-Computer Interaction</u>, in Donald A. Norman, Stephen W. Draper (ed.) Laurence Erlbaum Associates, Hillsdale, New Jersey and London, 1986, p. 93.
[4] Ibid., pp. 93, 94.
[5] Brenda Laurel, <u>Computers as Theatre</u>, Addison-Wesley Publishing Company, Reading, Massachusetts, 1991, p. xvi.
[6] John Frazer, <u>Themes VII: An Evolutionary Architecture</u>, Architectural Association Publications, London, 1995, p. 18.

LOFTING

Whilst waves convey the notion of liquidity as main characteristic of the digital domain, lofts propose a malleable, dense, oozy, more workable digital materiality. Within CAD software environments, 'lofts' are surfaces that pass through a series of curves, enabling the creation of open or closed entities. 'Periodic surfaces'[4] are closed surfaces (such as a cylindrical surface) that can be deformed without developing 'kinks'. Kinks, in comparison to knots, or control points of a spline, split the curve into multiple curves, and allow sharp, unsmooth edges along the spline. For the reason that (CAD) splines flow vectorially through their sequences of control points, they are "by definition continuous multiplicities rather than discrete entities"[5], as stated by Greg Lynn. Lynn describes multiplicities as a "continuous assemblage of heterogeneous singularities", representing a collection of heterogeneous components—without being reducible to neither the entity not the collection—that simultaneously displays "collective qualities of continuity and local qualities of heterogeneity".[6] The possibility of deformation of periodical surfaces into kink-free, smooth, fluid geometries oozing between splines conveys the notion of poetic automatism within the Baudrillardian idea of absolute singularity with infinite seriality.[7] Lofting builds upon the tradition of Surrealist 'psychic automatism', Gigeresque biomechanoids airbrushing, Miriam Cabessa's body paintings, and Roy Lichtenstein's dot matrix brush prints.

----

[4] Rhinoceros, copyright Robert McNeel & Associates.
[5] Greg Lynn, Animate Form, Princeton Architectural Press, New York, 1999, p. 23.
[6] Greg Lynn, Animate Form, Princeton Architectural Press, New York, 1999, p. 23.
[7] Jean Baudrillard, The System of Objects, trans. James Benedict, Verso, London and New York, 1996, p. 88.

[7] Karl S. Chu, The Turing Dimension.
[8] Piero Racanicchi, 'Mollino e la fotografia', [Il messaggio della camera oscura, C. Mollino, 1943], in Carlo Mollino 1905-1973, Documenti di Architettura, Electa, Turin. 1989, p. 70, trans. by the author.
[9] Jean Baudrillard, The System of Objects, trans. James Benedict, Verso, London and New York, 1996, p. 88.
[10] Ibid., p. 112.
[11] Ibid., p. 122.
[12] 'The Seminar of Jacques Lacan', in Book 11: The Ego in Freud's Theory and in the Technique of Psychoanalysis, Cambridge University Press, Cambridge, 1988, pp. 154-155.
[13] See Sherry Turkle, The Second Self: Computers and the Human Spirit, Simon & Schuster, New York, 1984.
[14] Žižek, pp. 122, 123.

System//Ontology

In the process of articulating an ontological model of an amenable rather than conflictual user-computer reflexive mimesis and symbiosis, the polite, dominant, mainstream stance of architecture students and professionals to think of the computer as a 'tool' has to be regarded as an irrational consideration. It is irrational given that it does not take into account, both in technological and in psychological terms, the rational aspects of computer systems and human models as researched by the discipline of Human-Computer Interaction. It is irrational as it reduces organisational skills and task related software architectures to data transfer processes, rather than complex symbolic manipulation operations. It is irrational because it sees the computer as a mere monolithic information machine, neglecting the interactive processes involved beyond its instrumental use, and, in Nicholas Negroponte's words, neglecting that "computer-aided design cannot occur without machine intelligence—and would be dangerous without it".[15] It is irrational for it does not recognize, as Gilles Deleuze states, that "the machine is always social before it is technical."[16] It is irrational, seeing that the 'thing' computer is an organ, as Henri Bergson claims, and a prosthetic entity necessary for controlling nature. It is irrational in view of the fact that it does not consider the computer as an "ideological artifice"[17], as Alicia Imperiale suggests. It is irrational since it demeans the computer to a mere object rather than a projective "fantasy screen", as it should, regarding to Slavoj Žižek.[18] It is irrational for the reason that the mind offers itself as model of the computer, as the computer offers itself as a model for the mind. It is irrational in the case the computer <u>was not</u> a thinking machine, since that would imply that also the self—a model of the computer—was not thinking, hence would be without reason. It is irrational in the case the computer <u>were</u> a thinking machine, since that would clash with the definition of tool as instrument. It is irrational on the basis that a tool has no motivation, no reason. It is irrational on account of a tool not being rational by itself. <u>Ergo, quod erat demonstrandum</u>, it is reasonable to say it is irrational; following Theodor Adorno's and Max Horkheimer's indication that "reason has become irrational".[19]

Under such designation, since the tool metaphor fails to explain the complex intrafacial framework as interactive, feedback driven, reflective mimetic intraface, how could such a system be described best? On one hand it cannot be dismissed that the intraface system's structure and evolutionary origin conveys fundamental properties that were postulated almost 60 years ago by Norbert Wiener in relationship to computers (and animals): communication, control, and feedback.[20] Later developed by James Licklider into the concept of 'formulative thinking'[21], his concepts have become a central field of study in the discipline of cybernetics, which relentlessly aims at improving data transfer (communication), behaviour theories (control) and optimisation (feedback). Here, as Michael Weinstock writes, "Feedback is understood as a kind of 'steering' device that regulates behaviour, using information from the environment to measure the actual performance against a desired or optimal performance."[22] Since the concept of interface is still rooted in the abstract Turing machine, it cannot represent from us intuitively perceived truth, but can nevertheless help us processing true intuitions.

Hence, intrafaces should not be misunderstood merely as an illustrator of calculated shapes, but as an <u>expression of formulated circumstances</u>, which require qualitative

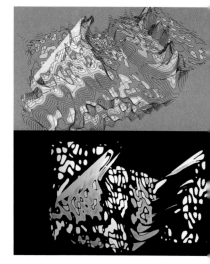

WAVES
As described by the Encyclopædia Britannica, an interface is a "surface separating two phases of matter" of a rather "thin layer that has properties differing from those of the bulk material on either side of the interface."[3] Waves appearing on surfaces identify the viscosity of fluids and liquids. Architects engaged with the advent of computers seem to have embarked on such a discourse, converging the terminology of describing virtual spaces towards fluidity: 'liquid', 'vacillating', 'oscillating', 'fluctuating', 'smooth', 'viscous', etc. Other architects, such as Volker Giencke (Egon), Reiser+Umemoto (Water Garden), Greg Lynn (Uniserve, I.F. NYC, Max Protech) and Mark Goulthorpe of dECOi (Aegis Hyposurface, wall in Haddad Apartments) to mention some, have also engaged with the aesthetics of wavy surfaces and gelatinous liquids.

- -
[3] <u>Interface</u>, Britannica© DVD 2000, Encyclopædia Britannica, Inc., 1994-1998.

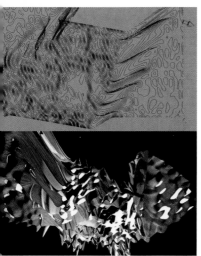

ROOF STRUCTURE OF FEIRA INTERNACIONAL
DOS AÇORES · MARCOSANDMARJAN · 2005

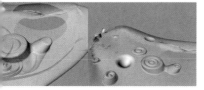

ROOF STRUCTURE OF NEW TOMIHIRO MUSEUM
MARCOSANDMARJAN · 2002

information rather than quantitative data. Under these circumstances, intrafaces exist in different phases and entail a twofold presence, for they remain intrinsic to the system, yet express coagulated information in their bounds. This expression of formulated circumstances is impulsive, intuitive, and reflexive. Markos Novak defines the term 'reflexive' as something suggesting 'self-reference and, consequently, a notion of self', which, he argues, introduced the discipline into "activity, transactivity, life and, eventually, consciousness" and as something suggesting "the reflective, the speculative and the conjectural". Reflexive architecture is hence alien architecture; the expression of a "great rewriting system that has provisions for freeing its outgrowths from the outmoded identities of its terra-bound roots as they branch across the n-dimensional terrain of unexplored variables and unexpected but inevitable combinations."[23]

Hence, the tectonics of the convoluted field, in which homologous intrafaces flourish, is best expressed with the concept of splinear fabric. For the reason that splines (a 'spline' being a computer-generated curvilinear line defined by minimum 3 points) flow vectorially through their sequences of control points, they are described by Greg Lynn in Animate Form as "continuous multiplicities rather than discrete entities", the former themselves being a "continuous assemblage of heterogeneous singularities", and representing a collection of heterogeneous components—without being reducible to neither the entity not the collection—that simultaneously displays "collective qualities of continuity and local qualities of heterogeneity".[24] Borrowing from mathematician Andre Linde's and Lynn's terminology, it may be stated that 'interactable' elements in the bounds of the digital 'existence' realm of intrafaces are possible because of their 'flexible topological' expressions within spline-controlled systems.

Inside the realm of homologous, mimetic, convoluted, splinear intrafaces, a very particular species of digital entities can exist and breed in adequate software territories.

'Splinimals' can best be described as a crossbreed—between splines (interpolated curves that flow between and are animated by knots or control points) and animals—that inhabit the domain of digitally constructed space. Hybrid entities as they are, Splinimals can be understood as quintessential 'animate forms', a term of course borrowed again from architect Greg Lynn. As he suggests, the term animation "implies the evolution of a form and its shaping forces; it suggests animalism, animism, growth, actuation, vitality and virtuality"[25]. Splinimals possess all these animate characteristics, and due to their splinear traits, they are on the whole amenable, docile, interactable and easily approachable, surviving in the bounds of Wiener's parameters of communication, control, and feedback. In a hypothetical equation where Lynn's animate forms are linked to his understanding of the computer being considered a 'pet'[26] due to its domestication into the discipline of architecture, Splinimals would find their counterpart in my understanding of the computer as a soft toy, attributable to their extreme level of animism, interaction, reflexive association, emotional symbiosis, and blissful mimesis. Challenging the futile idea of computer as mere technological, Kantian noumenal, intelligible 'thing', intraface enacts within the user a higher degree of associative assessment towards machines. Moving away from the Heideggerian imprisonment of technology dominated by the definition of engagement as 'calculative thinking', the soft toy-computer enables what Neil Leach refers to as "an unconscious identification with the object"[27]: that 'appropriation' that involves a process of 'familiarisation' with places, objects, scenarios etc., in other words the Freudian 'symbolic attachment'[28] process happening over time.

- -

[15] Nicholas Negroponte, The Architecture Machine. Toward a More Human Environment, The MIT Press, Cambridge Massachusetts and London, 1970, p. 1.
[16] Gilles Deleuze and Claire Parnet, Dialogues, London, 1977, pp. 126-7.
[17] Alicia Imperiale, New Flatness - Surface Tension in Digital Architecture, Birkhäuser, Basel, Boston, Berlin, 2000, p. 75.
[18] Žižek, p. 123.
[19] Theodor Adorno and Max Horkheimer, Philosophical Fragments, 1944.
[20] Norbert Wiener, Cybernetics, or Control and Communication in the Animal and the Machine, MIT Press, Cambridge Massachusetts, 1961.

DRAPES

Drape projects a surface over meshes, surfaces, and solids. As drapes use the points' location in the "render depth buffer (z-buffer)"[8] as value for the drapes' control points, it behaves 'ergonomically' towards the splinear fabric of the convoluted field.

By definition, the terms flatness and surface, as argued by Alicia Imperiale in New Flatness, connote two distinctive concepts: the first refers to the plane "on which future architectures are projected", may it be paper or a computer screen; the latter refers to the envelope and depth of the architecture itself.[9] By geometrical description, flatness and surface are also to be distinguished: absolute flat geometrical drawings employ a zero value on the z-axis of the Cartesian X, Y, Z point coordinates system projected by the software; on the other hand, NURBS (Non-Uniform Rational Bézier Spline) surfaces are constructed out of splines sequences, and are expresses by flat, directional U, V values.

Although Greg Lynn believes that only forms constructed in a parametrical computer-aided design concept employ the linkages between the characteristics of the "three fundamental properties of organization"[10] in animate digital forms— topology, time, and parameters—necessary to conceive animate rather than static space, the counterargument brought forward by Bernard Cache that "topology (the development of surfaces) is actually incorporated within the system of Euclidean geometry"[11], may enrich the architectural language beyond curvilinear, rolling, and smooth NURBS surfaces. Nevertheless, Lynn is right in challenging the designer into understanding topological patterns in their dynamic unfolding and varying performance, rather merely as shapes.

[8] Rhinoceros, copyright Robert McNeel & Associates.

[9] Alicia Imperiale, New Flatness - Surface Tension in Digital Architecture, Birkhäuser, Basel, Boston, Berlin, 2000, p. 5.

[10] Greg Lynn, Animate Form, Princeton Architectural Press, New York, 1999, p. 20.

[11] Alicia Imperiale, New Flatness - Surface Tension in Digital Architecture, Birkhäuser, Basel, Boston, Berlin, 2000, p. 77.

DRAPING OF FLL FOLIES
MARCOSANDMARJAN · 2005

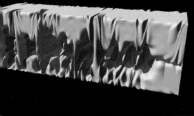

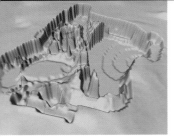

DRAPING OF EXHIBITION CRATERS
FEIRA INTERNACIONAL DOS AÇORES
MARCOSANDMARJAN · 2005

[21] James R. Licklider, ‚Man-Computer Symbiosis', in IRE Transactions on Human Factors in Electronics, March 1960, quoted in Wurster, p. 285.

[22] Michael Weinstock, 'Morphogenesis and the Mathematics of Emergence', pp. 10-17, in Michael Hensel, Achim Menges and Michael Weinstock (guest.ed.), Emergence: Morphogenetic Design Strategies, Architectural Design Vol 74 No 3, Wiley-Academy, London, 2004, p. 13.

[23] Marcos Novak, 'Transvergence, Allogenesis: Notes on the Production of the Alien', pp. 64-71, in Neil Spiller (guest-ed.), Reflexive Architecture, Architectural Design Vol 72 No 3, Wiley-Academy, London, 2002, p. 65.

[24] Greg Lynn, Animate Form, Princeton Architectural Press, New York, 1999, p. 23.

[25] Ibid., p. 9.

[26] Ibid., pp. 19-20.

[27] Neil Leach (ed.), Designing For A Digital World, Wiley-Academy, with RIBA Future Studies, Chichester, 2001, p. 26.

[28] Ibid., p. 25.

Disembodiment//Architecture//Phenomenology

On a phenomenological level, man-computer symbiosis has to move swiftly past the Cyborgian vision of reinterpreted Victorian automata towards software based metatechnological sensory and sensual digitality, where in Stephen Perella's words the "metaphorical becomes haptic."[29]

According to philosopher Henri Bergson, it is human intelligence and animal instinct that direct life towards things; and it is a particular tendency of the human intellect to render things as prostheses of the body, thus to humanise and control nature.[30] In accordance, Grosz claims that this prosthesis of inorganic matter "transformed into an immense organ," resembles the "primordial or elementary definition of architecture itself."[31] In this sense architecture is the 'first prosthesis' to the human intellect in melding the world 'into things'. Heidegger, who demands "essential reflection upon technology and decisive confrontation" with technology in a domain which is both similar yet essentially different, believes architecture to be such a realm; for it is both similar yet essentially different to the domain of technology."
As Grosz argues, technology then is that, which negotiates between the world of things and the body.[32] Throughout this negotiation between the thing, the intellect, the body, perception and technology, something is nonetheless not addressed, which Grosz describes as the "object of intuition, of empirical attunement without means or ends"[33]—that which is not exploited, not practical, not useful, not human.

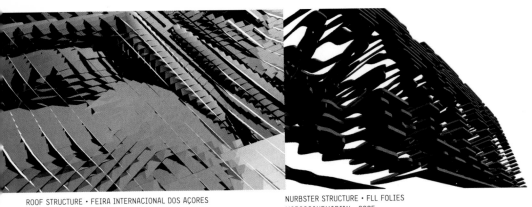

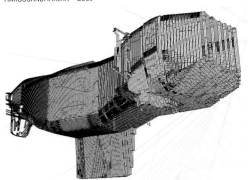

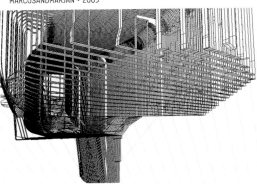

ROOF STRUCTURE · FEIRA INTERNACIONAL DOS AÇORES
MARCOSANDMARJAN · 2005

NURBSTER STRUCTURE · FLL FOLIES
MARCOSANDMARJAN · 2005

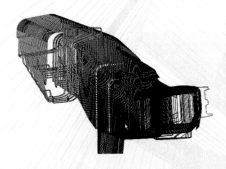

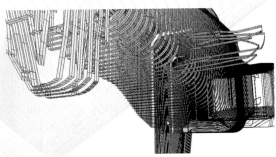

STRUCTURAL STUDIES OF FLOATING VESSEL
NEW GODET CLUB
MARCOSANDMARJAN · 2003

In the essay <u>Escape from the Revolving Door: Architecture and the Machine</u>, Robert McCarter explicates his concern with the "propensity of utilitarian and economic determinism' in his time, the so-called 'information age".[34] McCarter questions the way technological thinking is conceived. Technological thinking, in a Bergsonian approach, presumes an intentionality of control and domination over nature, and thus, in a Heideggerian understanding, over man himself, as being and having nature himself. In such a state of thinking, being consists of being '<u>usable</u>'.[35] The means (to some ends) of technology then become, by definition, ends in themselves.

SECTIONING
The (serial) cuts resulting on NURBS surfaces and volumes are splines. In relationship to the capability of the homologous, mimetic intraface to produce poetic automatism, the automatism involved in sectioning and contouring surfaces and volumes in 3D software environments may express the status of synthesising "absolute singularity" with "infinite seriality"[12] explicated by Baudrillard. Under such circumstances the CAD created series of sections allow complexity yet retain parameters of compatibility and continuity. Within the general interpretation of complexity, as Andrew Benjamin writes, it is the 'Cartesian heritage' of complexity that identifies the possibility of the complex.[13]

- -

[12] Jean Baudrillard, The System of Objects, trans. James Benedict, Verso, London and New York, 1996, p. 88.
[13] Andrew Benjamin (ed.), Complexity – Architecture / Art / Philosophy, Journal of Philosophy and the Visual Art No 6, Academy Editions, London, 1995, p. 7.

At the end of the 19th century, the fourth largest city in Europe, Vienna, was experiencing a considerable flourishing of artistic and intellectual potential. Sigmund Freud, Otto Wagner, Gustav Mahler and Arnold Schönberg, just to mention a few, played an important role in the increasing engagement with not only the traditional and the modern, but also with reality and illusion. As the Viennese Secession was influenced by the newly discovered, parallel reality of the unconscious and the mind, modern architects and artists are similarly excited by the newly created, parallel reality of the cyberspace and virtual reality. Likewise, both psychoanalysis and technology re-introduced a dualistic view of space. Psychoanalysis and its conscious-unconscious separation followed the strict monolithic, absolute definition of space by scientists: Newton, building up on Kepler's work, ultimately unified and equalized terrestrial and celestial space through the law of gravity, which, by operating in the very same matter in both realms, implied matter in the celestial heavens too. One century later, cyberspace and its virtual reality are following the again strict monolithic, physician, absolute definition of space by scientists: Einstein, Hawking and the 'theorists of everything' describe an invisible, ethereal substance or space, not surrounding objects, but being them. This modern definition of the so-called 'hyperspace' unifies and equalizes everything, time and space included, to a homogeneous, total real, with several mathematical equations such as matter or even God. Throughout history, 'stereo' and 'mono' understandings of space have alternated each other; and annihilations of the celestial, spiritual, res cogitans realm have predominantly been initiated by great astronomers known for their breakthrough in the understanding of the Heavens: Ptolemy, Copernicus, Galilei, Kepler, Newton, Hubble, Einstein, Hawking.

Because the computer's evolutionary path was mostly drafted by mathematicians, it was developed as machine that would enable them to have insight into complex systems of mathematical or biological nature. Turing himself, in fact, had a lifelong interest in the geometric and mathematical principles inherent to the morphogenesis—the evolutionary (over time) creation of forms—of plants.[37] Both he and Von Neumann, who played major roles in the development of the computer, were interested in producing a machine capable of duplicating both mathematical as well as natural functions.[37]

In this sense, ontological evolutionary properties of computers have also emerged into phenomenological evolutionary designs of CAD architectures. As much as Enlightenment endeavoured to find mechanistic and political parallels between machines and bodies, the contemporary architectural debate, both within theory and praxis, delineates a working concept for the discipline (especially because embedded in, and supported by, CAD technologies) based on the observation and simulation of complex, morphogenetic systems towards emergence. In recent history, it is these terms that have led most of the architectural theories and designs.

From the observation of morphogenetic system, two branches of architectural mindsets seem to have arisen. A first, analogue approach finds expression in organic architecture; a second, later digital strand divulges mathematical, and algorithmic (term derived from Persian mathematician al-Hwarizmi, †850) working concepts.

TWOANDAHALF DIMENSION

The infinite digital space formed in computer-aided design can most precisely be described by splinear, twoandahalfdimensional drawings that convey more convolute spatial attributes than simple two-dimensional line drawings, yet less than three-dimensional NURBS entities. Although twoandahalf-dimensional drawings remain infinitely flat geometrical drawings, they appear spatial in the manifestation of surfaces, volumes and shadows. The twoandahalfdimensional architecture of digital space should not be understood merely as an illustration of calculated shapes, but as an expression of formulated circumstances, which do not require quantitative data, but rather qualitative information.

Embedded in mathematical calculus, twoandahalf-dimensional computer-aided design can develop infinite space that can be computationally built, and that allow the qualification of specific information, save for its quantification. The likelihood of interactable multiplicities that present specific qualifiable yet not quantifiable information must be accepted in the same way as the option of null, zero, nought, to exist as possibility for a positive number. In mathematical terms, some properties of such existence spaces can be described with help of Georg Cantor's argument of the 'transfinite numbers'. The mathematician argued that beyond the natural series of finite numbers, 1, 2, 3, 4, 5, 6, 7, 8, 9, 10, 11, 12, 13, ..., n,...., one could designate any symbol as being a number. Then, according to the secondaxiom of G. Peano, if the symbol is a number, also the symbol+1 is a number, and therefore symbol+2 is also a number etc. According to Cantor, the symbol is greater than all finite numbers, and is the first 'transfinite ordinal number'.[14] The series would therefore look like, with ω as symbol:

$$1, 2, 3,..., \omega, \omega +1, \omega +2, \omega + 3,...,$$
$$\omega 2, \omega 2 + 1, \omega 2 + 2, \omega.2 + 3,..., \omega.3,...,$$
$$\omega 2. ... ,\omega^\omega, ... ,\omega^{\omega^\omega}, ... ,\omega^{\omega^{\omega^\omega}} \quad (=\varepsilon_0)$$

Of course, in Rose's terms, the symbol
must also be required not to disappear
when it goes to zero-content.

- -

[14] Alexander Alexandrovich Zenkin, Whether
God exists in the Transfinite Paradise of Georg
Cantor?, in the Journal News of Artificial Intelligence, #1,
p.156-160 (in Russian).

DIGITAL STUDY
MARJAN COLLETTI • 2003

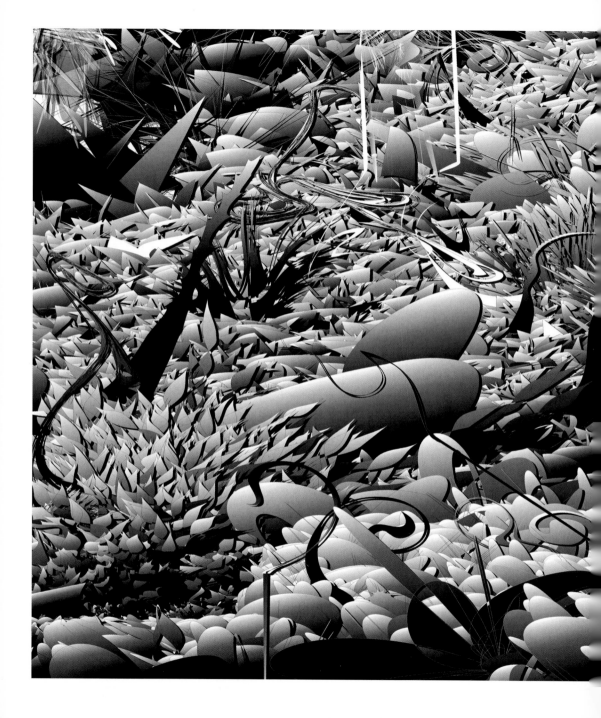

2&1/2D #54 "AVATAR" • MARJAN COLLETTI • 2004

The work of marcosandmarjan, and of Marcos and Marjan individually, tends to lean towards the former expression of architecture. On the digital platform, the working methodology repossesses previous, almost anthroposophic, ideas. Embedded in anthroposophic ideas, architecture represented to Rudolf Steiner the discipline that engages the most with the three main factors of human life: movement, feelings, and thoughts. Thus explains Vittorio Leti Messina in Rudolf Steiner. Architetto: Architecture must deal with the aspects of movement in ways of managing technological, economical, scientific, technical issues related to Man as 'physical inhabitant'. On the other hand, the architect can act artistically since the aspects of emotions demand aesthetic consideration of forms, colours, and rhythms. Finally, the factor of thoughts truly defines the role of the architect: here, the architect can communicate concepts (the naming of a perception) and ideas (where intuition meets perception) with means of representations.[38]

Especially in consideration of how Virtual Reality and Cybernetics have brought forth a belief in the complete disembodiment of cyberspace, almost culminating in a quasi-religious myth of total liberation from physical limitations, the architectural design and research work here presented, both on Mimetic Intrafaces and Inhabitable Interfaces, endeavours to integrate quasi-anthroposophic ideas of movement (body), feelings (soul), and thoughts (psyche) into a (possibly) built quasi-technocratic vision of communication, control, and feedback.

What is noticeable in the production of digital design within the last decade is a precarious drift towards the psychosis described by Pierre Janet as 'legendary psychasthenia'[39]. In psychasthenia, the impossibility of the interlinking of subject, body and objects occurs in a psychotic definition and representation of space, where the imaginary body, the ego, and the existence fails to locate and represent themselves. Against this development of utterly reducing architectural vocabulary to surface, parameters, emergence, process... marcosandmarjan include several functional yet

DIGITAL ORNAMENT//BLURRINESS
If digital architectural vocabulary is to be developed beyond already existing terminology the creative use of the computer must allow the rise of a-parametrical, non-algorithmic, post-evolutionary aesthetics. The switch from digital tectonics to digital ornamentation is imminent, and would allow the typological advancement of interfaces to intrafaces, as discussed in the essay.

I find it difficult to disagree with Hugo Häring: 'functional forms' are identical all over the world and history, while 'expressive forms' are 'dependent on time and place' and bound by Blood (German Blut) and Knowledge (German Erkenntnis);[15] or with Carlo Mollino: If technology loses its direction, it is estranged and alienated from man, and objects are produced only to be used and consumed; or with Arendt: Experience needs to replace mere information. If means—utility—replace meanings, meaninglessness is generated.[16] Once under the sphere of influence of functionality, technology fails from being experienced, and, as Theodor Adorno predicted, it can only be 'operated'. To Mollino the progression of technologies and techniques continuously places at man's disposal new pretexts and hence ways/methods of expression, even if those technologies are not directly intended to produce poetry.[17] McCarter demands confrontation and opposition, which are to come 'from within'; from architecture; from the research into "more original relationships between man and technology; through rediscovery of experimental and inventive technological creation; and through re-engagement of technology and experience in the making of tectonic form.'[18]

- -

[15] David Pearson, new organic architecture - the breaking wave, Gaia Books Limited, London, 2001, pp. 43, 44.
[16] Ibid., p. 10.
[17] Elena Tamagno, 'L'archivio Carlo Mollino. Testimonianze di un quarantennio di vita', pp. 107-113, in Carlo Mollino 1905-1973, Documenti di
Architettura, Electa, Turin, 1989, p.109, transl. by the author.
[18] McCarter, p. 12.

descriptive factors into a design's agenda: materiality, inhabitation, volumetric geometry, ornamentation, ergonomics….

- -

[29] Stephen Perrella, 'Hypersurface architecture and the question of interface', Interfacing Realities, http://framework.v2.nl/archive/archive/node/text/default.xslt/nodenr-70021
[30] Henri Bergson, Creative Evolution, trans. Arthur Mitchell, Random House, New York.
[31] Elizabeth Grosz, Architecture from the Outside: Essays on Virtual and Real Space, The MIT Press Cambridge Massachusetts and London England, 2001, p. 178.
[32] Ibid., p. 182.
[33] Ibid., p. 183.
[34] Robert McCarter (ed.), Pamphlet Architecture N.12- Building; Machines, Pamphlet Architecture and Princeton Architectural Press, New York, 1987, pp. 7-12.
[35] Ibid., p. 8.
[36] Michael Weinstock, 2004, p. 14.
[37] John Frazer, 1995, p. 13.
[38] Vittorio Leti Messina, Rudolf Steiner. Architetto, Universale di architettura #11, collana diretta da Bruni Zevi, Testo & Immagine, Torino, 1996, pp. 17, 18, transl. by the auhor.
[39] Elizabeth Grosz, 2001, pp. 38.

MEDUSA

A BLANKET FOR THE SOFT TOYS, 1998.

Project description:
Medusa, like the Greek mythological
figure, tends to freeze observers.
It presents the soft toys and their
cuteness and softness as part of an
architectural thesis and conviction.
A soft blanket allows the wrapping
around, and housing of several soft
toys. A grid of Velcro tape represents
the soft structure of the blanket, which
thus can be folded in all possible ways.
The blanket is then velcroed onto the
architect's shaved head. The resulting friendly wig resembles a baroque
hairstyle, and introduces the notion of
ornament into the work.
The fragmentation of the line into a
written text conveys the notion of softness and endeavours to comment the
hard lined attitude of folds and trian-
gulation in recent digital architecture
- - - - - - - - - - - - - - - - - - - -
Programme:
'Housing' several soft toys in a portable
'dwelling'.
- - - - - - - - - - - - - - - - - - - -
Team:
M. Colletti, (supervised by Yael Reisner
and Peter Cook).

BESKING

A HYBRID BETWEEN A BED+DESK+THING,
1999.

Project description:
Several elements, build up the Besking:
water carrying pipes hold together
by the endless wrapping, unbalanced
legs stabilized by the messy carpet,
the architect's and the guest's seat,
the inflatable blanket, the Easter-gar-
den and a pump that allows water to
run through the pipes creating diver-
gence zones of different temperatures
and allowing movements of the different elements. All these elements have
a 'double personality': the pipes are
major element but rather wild, the legs
are adjustable but unstable, the carpet
is light but messy, the blanket is soft
but shy, the architect' seat is adaptable
yet unmovable whilst the guest's seat
is funny but naughty.
The Besking includes two different
scales, the human scale and the soft
toys scale. In fact, in all the
drawings—plans, sections, elevations,
details—the friendly soft toys re-appear
in the shapes of the Besking: there are
polar bears, seals, whales, elephants,
huskys in the section, lions, whales,
seals, and myself, in the plans etc.
The curvilinearity of the design hints at
research into the splinear fabric of convoluted fields, playing with ornamented
CAD lines, some of them resulting from
interfering with software commands.
- - - - - - - - - - - - - - - - - - - -
Programme:
1 bed, 1 desk, 1 seat for the architect,
1 seat for guests, flower pot, lamp,
trash bin, drawers, plan holders etc.
- - - - - - - - - - - - - - - - - - - -
Team:
M. Colletti, (supervised by Yael Reisner
and Peter Cook).

BASKING

A HOUSE IN HAMPSTEAD · LONDON, 1999.

Project description:
Situated next to the London park Hampstead Heath, the house for the Profes-
sional Architect basks relaxed in its
own Garden, enjoying the admiration
of passers-by. All over the site, an
artificial meadow—a water filled rub-
ber-mattress which keeps memory of
the way people walk on it—tells the
people that they stand on private prop-
erty. Blurring the boundaries between
the inside and the outside of the building, soft walls and inflatable doors,
vegetation and waterfalls, and a series
of footpaths separate and/or join and
define the spaces.
A floating swimming pool, like a hu-
mungous flower, grows out of the garden
and blossoms regularly, changing its
shape depending on the season. Water
can be pumped through its double-
layered skin in order to calibrate the
pool's shape: from open in the summer
to enclosed in the winter. An ic-exibi-
tion, an artificial forest of ice, allows
the architect to exhibit his work, but
keeps people away as a consequence of
its unfriendly atmosphere. Cypresses,
often planted close to private villas in
northern Italy, grow out of highly light-
reflecting, earth-filled fabric bags,
which act as columns for the translucent roof.
- - - - - - - - - - - - - - - - - - - -
Programme:
Bus station, private dwelling, terrace,
garden with pond and waterfall, exhibition space, swimming pool.
- - - - - - - - - - - - - - - - - - - -
Team:
M. Colletti, (supervised by Yael Reisner
and Peter Cook).

BLURSKING

FLAT REFURBISHMENT, BOLZANO/BOZEN
ITALY, 2000 · (BLURRED SKIN) + (LIVING
AS KING).

Project description:
The refurbishment project of a flat in
Bolzano/Bozen Italy engages in the
research undertaken on 'softness' and
'blurriness'. Partly sanded glass walls
act as physical partitions of functions,
yet link the spaces together in a blurred
and soft perception of a whole environment. Here, the wall is considered a
screen. Rather than blocking the view,
the screen allows the gaze into spaces
semi-visible behind the blurry wall;
they monitor events and light conditions
and display them to the other side,
affecting that space as well. The body
vanishes into blurriness, fake reflec-
tions trigger curiosity and refractions
add layers and layers of details that
create a 'cloudy' and 'soft' experience
of the space and of the walls.
Other horizontal elements cut through
functions and spaces merging them.
They perform the major infrastructural
functions of the flat, and soften the
rigidity of boundary conditions, whilst
relating two spaces contemporarily.
- -

Programme:
Flat refurbishment: kitchen, bathroom,
shower room/wc, living room, bedroom.
- -

Team:
M. Colletti.

SARAJEVO FROM THE ASHES

THE NEW IDENTITY MUSEUM OF POST-WAR
SARAJEVO, 1997.

Project description:
The New Identity Museum represents
Part II of a total urban redevelopment
of wounded post-war Sarajevo that
considers the complex socio-political
urban environment of the city.
The design explores the possibility
of anthropomorphism, organic architecture, experimental structures, inside-
outside boundary conditions, and mixed
inhabitation of complex geometries.
- -

Programme:
Museum, internal and external exhibition space, auditorium, Mediatheque,
restaurant, bookshop.
- -

Team:
M. Colletti (supervised by Volker
Giencke).

CLOUD

A BALLROOM PROJECT FOR THE CITY OF
BOLZANO/BOZEN · ITALY, 1995.

Project description:
The 'Cloud' proposes a series of floating decks inside a double, inflatable,
translucent resin membrane, hold by a
series of inclined columns, that acts
as 'screws' for fixing the lightweight
structure into the ground, taking into
account the grid of the existing underground parking.
Nicknamed the 'Cloud' due to its organic
shape, and its lightweight structure,
the projects embarks on topics that are
later constantly readdressed in marcosandmarjan projects, such as organic
architecture, translucent membranes,
softness and curvilinearity, experimental and flexible structures, digital
ornamentation, inhabitation.
- -

Programme:
Ballroom, several restaurants, exhibition spaces.
- -

Team:
M. Colletti, Sonja Mitterer (supervised
by Volker Giencke).

Floating Vessel

Project for the New Godet Club, Istanbul Turkey, 2003

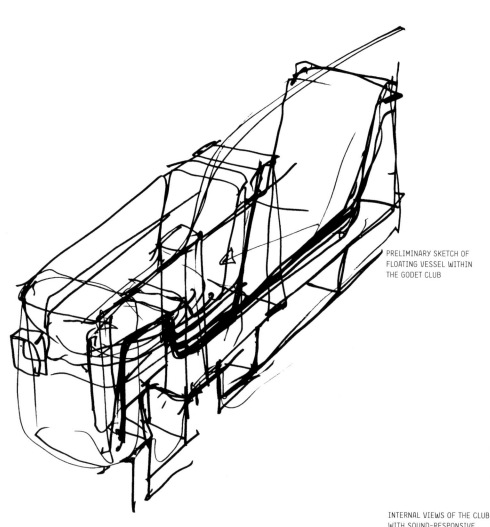

PRELIMINARY SKETCH OF
FLOATING VESSEL WITHIN
THE GODET CLUB

INTERNAL VIEWS OF THE CLUB
WITH SOUND-RESPONSIVE
SCREEANS AND PRESSURE-
-SENSITIVE FLOOR CUSHIONS

GENERAL VIEW WITH FLOATING VESSEL, DIGITAL CURTAINS, AND SUSPENDED DJ-CAPSULE

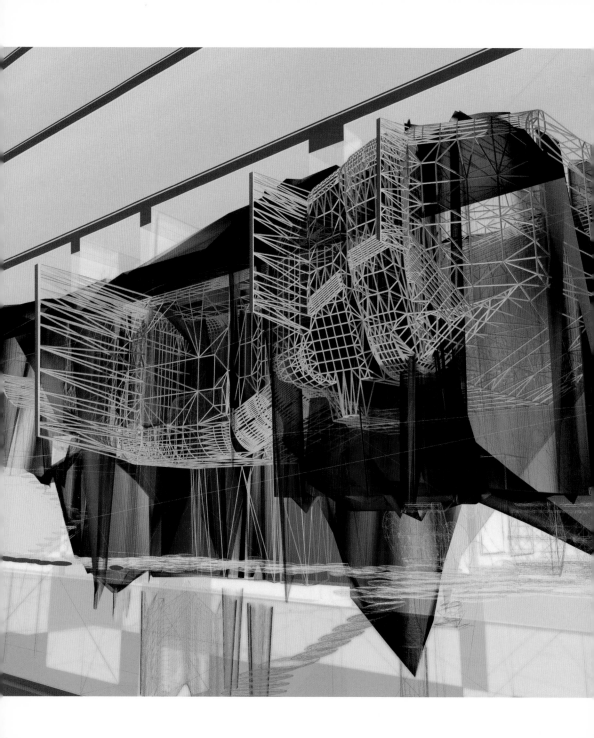

PLAN OF FLOATING VESSEL
AND DIGITAL CURTAINS

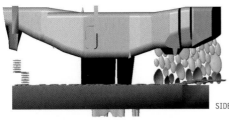

SIDE ELEVATION

FRONTAL ELEVATION
WITH DJ CAPSULE

STUDY OF SOUND-RESPONSIVE SCREENS

FLOATING VESSEL
DETAILED LATEX MODEL OF 'INLUCENT' SKIN

STUDY OF DIGITAL
CURTAINS

Team » Design: marcosandmarjan › Collaborators: Jia Lu

- -

The Godet Club is located in the Beyoglu district of Istanbul, an area with predominantly European-style nineteenth century housing and the centre for entertainment and nightlife. The club is situated just off Istiklal Cadesi, the main shopping street of Istanbul, and is proposed as a new centre for innovative and experimental multimedia activities in the city. The programmatic organisation of the club into differentiated acoustic areas triggers the concept of a "Floating Vessel", an enclosed chill-out lounge hovering over the noisy open areas of entrance, bar and dance floors. The external presence of this vessel is given by a protruding DJ-capsule on the existing street elevation. The transparent and informative façade is an interface that partly reveals to the exterior the internal activities of the club. The interior shows an "inlucent" materiality: a translucent resin membrane incorporates the structure, technical appliances, robotic devices, and audio-visual equipment exposing itself as the visible "vascular system" of the club. In the entrance floor pressure-sensitive resin cushions change the luminosity and colour saturation according to the variable space occupation. On the dance floor flexible flat screens are sound-responsive and linked to the internet. On the walls a series of monitor vessels react to the air quality creating an ever-changeable pattern of biological matter*.

*The biological monitors were designed and produced by Steve Pike during his studies in Unit 20 at the Bartlett School of Architecture UCL. Dr. Conrad Mullineaux at the Micro-biology Department and Dr. Richard Strange at the Mycology Department, both at University College London, technically supervised the whole process. After being installed in the Godet Club they would need regular maintenance and control by scientists from laboratories at the University of Istanbul.

75ª Feira do Livro de Lisboa

Project for the 75th Lisbon Book Fair, Lisbon Portugal, 2005

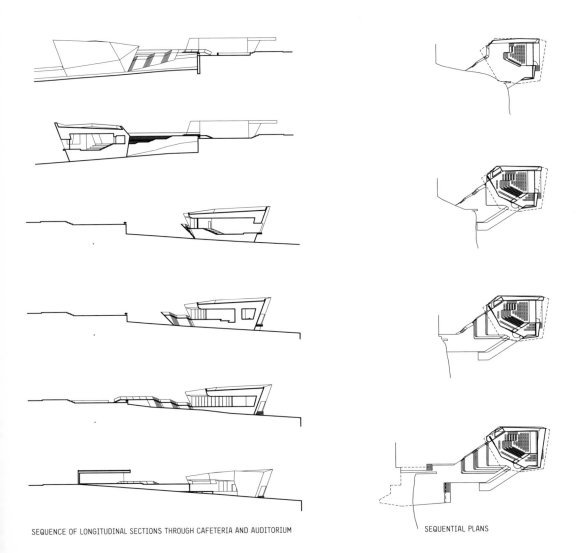

SEQUENCE OF LONGITUDINAL SECTIONS THROUGH CAFETERIA AND AUDITORIUM

SEQUENTIAL PLANS

AERIAL VIEW WITH LOCATION OF CAFETEIRA, AUDITORIUM, INFO PAVILION
AND SITTING FOLIES ON THE NORTH SIDE OF PARQUE EDUARDO VII

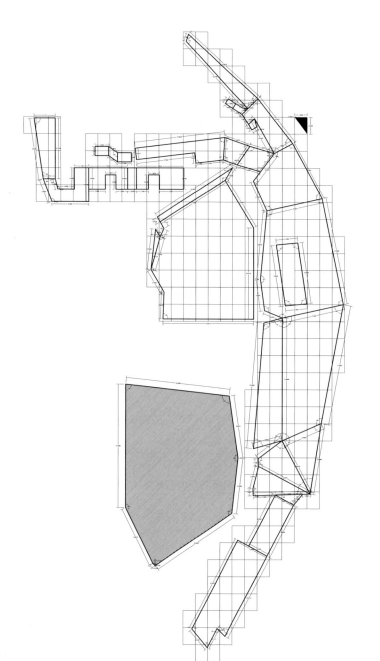

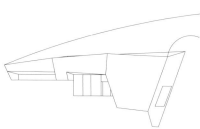

UNFOLDED SURFACES OF AUDITORIUM FACADE

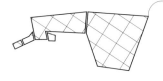

Client » Câmara Municipal de Lisboa, EGEAC › Team » Design: marcosandmarjan › Collaborators: João Albuquerque, Shui Liu, Marco Sacchi › Associate Architects: Guedes & Viinikainen › Associate Engineer: Francisco Bernardo – A400 › Graphic Design: Barbara Says › Laser Cutting: Lasindústria › Construction: Contubos › Contrstruction cost: 500.000.00 Euros › Programme: General layout of Book Fair, Cafeteria, Auditorium, Outside Esplanade, Information Pavilion › Total construction area: 1000m²

- -

The 75th Lisbon Book Fair is characterised by a variety of spaces and atmospheres to be discovered while walking along the Boulevards on both sides of the Parque Eduardo VII. Against the traditional layout of stands and pavilions aligned in parallel rows, this proposal's organisation positions the stands around several open areas in order to form small squares with a strong urban feeling. These spaces are differentiated by their spatial arrangement and colour, being simultaneously resting spaces, and areas where specific activities for the publishers can take place.

The access to fair is permitted from different sides and punctuated by main public pavilions. But it is on the north side that the most iconographic infrastructures are implanted: the information pavilion on the top of the eastern boulevard, and the cafeteria and auditorium on the top of the western boulevard; the last one being a structure that is projected from the street level down to the middle of the park.

The architecture project that accompanies the fair integrates a 1000m2 construction of three independent structures: an auditorium for a minimum of 150 people, a self-service cafeteria with an exterior esplanade for 70 people and an information pavilion. Differently form other years, the proposal links the auditorium and the cafeteria through a large staircase, which allows the seating area of the auditorium to be extended to the outside. This solution of a created amphitheatre permits the users of the cafeteria to watch the cultural activities inside the auditorium, while appreciating the views over the city from the outside or through the large window opening behind the stage. This auditorium can host not just the cultural events linked to the book fair, as well as have concerts or theatre performances that can be enjoyed from the outside when the sliding doors are opened during the warm summer nights. It later became re-entitled as 'Sky Lounge' and reutilised as a high level club for special events in the park during the following summer months.

The sculptural expression of the building publishes the inner events through its strong visual impact in the surrounding landscape: the bar announces the fair through a cantilever, which is projected over the pavement of the street; the auditorium is extended down into the green area right into the middle of the park. It is visible from a great distance, such as the Avenida da Liberdade or even from the S. Jorge castle. The volume of the auditorium is characterised through a sequence of inclined red surfaces, into which

CONSTRUCTION OF AUDITORIUM AND CAFETERIA WITH SCAFFOLDING STRUCTURE AND MDF CLADDING

© Virgilio Ferreira

EAST VIEW OF AUDITORIUM WITH ILLUMINATED LOGO

NORTH VIEW OF CAFETERIA ENTRANCE

PANORAMIC VIEW FROM HIGHEST POINT OF PARQUE EDUARDO VII

the logo of the fair is laser cut. This volume is central to the whole fair and accessible from three sides, with various perspectival conditions, as if it were three distinct buildings.

The structure is nick named 'lizard' because of the way in which it lies in the topography of the park (original project by architect Keil do Amaral during the years of the Portuguese dictatorship) and how it overviews the city. The diagonal disposition of the structure and its strong horizontality reinforces the wish to break the symmetry of the park and stands in contrast to the vertical presence of the pre-exiting columns, nevertheless incorporating them into the overall design.

Due to the temporary nature of the building and the speed of its construction (4 weeks), as well as the impossibility to ground it with foundations, the construction was quickly assembled with a scaffolding structure surrounded by an exterior mdf cladding, both of which to be reutilised.

The three-dimensional complexity of the building topography forced the process to be determined by intensive 3D computer modelling, afterwards controlled by 2D drawings illustrating a large series of sequential sections and plans.

SOUTHWEST VIEW

INTERNAL VIEW OF AUDITORIUM WITH LISBON IN THE BACKGROUND

VIEW OF AUDITORIUM AND PARQUE EDUARDO VII
WITH COLUMN OF MARQUES DO POMBAL AND RIVER
TEJO IN THE BACKGROUND

INHABITABLE INTERFACES
by <u>Marcos Cruz</u>

<u>Inhabitable Interfaces</u> is, as an initial formulation,
a phenomenon that is explored through a conceptual
switch from a traditional space-centric understanding of
architecture to a wall-centric understanding of space. It is
clear that the conventional design of space has been mainly
concerned with the use and organisation of 'empty' space
– and walls have been socially, politically and functionally
relegated and 'restricted' as mere space dividers. Yet, there
is more to say to about what is actually hidden behind our
contemporary physical surrounding. Therefore it is important
to question the contemporary relationship between the
human body, walls and the space we inhabit. Historically,
one observes a shift from conventional space inhabitation to
more contemporary wall inhabitation, in which 'inhabitable'
is a condition that is ever transient and implies the
potential act of becoming inhabited. Contemporary concepts
of inhabitation are challenged by the physical and virtual
expansion of our human perception and, as <u>William
Mitchell</u> refers in his book <u>City of Bits</u>, are taking on a new
meaning, that "has less to do with parking your bones in an
architecturally defined space and more with connecting your
nervous system to nearby electronic organs. Your room and
your home [and your walls] will become part of you, and you
will become part of them."[1]

What is defined as an <u>Inhabitable Interface</u> in architecture
embodies a wider understanding of wall as a "primary
architectural state"[2]: It stands in opposition to the common and

NURBSTER IV WITH INCORPORATED SITTING
FACILITY AND NETWORKED DIGITAL INTERFACE
FENG CHIA & BARTLETT DIGITAL ARCHITECTURE
WORKSHOP · TAICHUNG TAIWAN · 2005

reductive metaphor of 'skin' that <u>Adrian Forty</u> recognised has for long been used to define walls as flat and thin membrane-like conditions, denying them the virtue of thick walls[3].
And this is true, in particular, in a time where a pervasive digital discourse is making the architectural skin ever thinner and more transparent, simultaneously risking to disembody it further from architecture. On the contrary, there is an increasing value in the notion of thick embodied wall interfaces that encompass new corporeal qualities in architecture.

- -

[1] William Mitchell: <u>City of Bits - Space, Place and the Infobahn</u>, MIT Press, 1996 (p. 30)
[2] Peter Wood: <u>Sticks and Stones: Skins and Bones</u> in <u>AD - Surface Consciousness</u> (ed. Mark Taylor) Vol. 73 No.2 March/April 2003 (p. 66)
[3] Adrian Forty: <u>Inside the Whale</u> in Laura Allen, Iain Borden, Peter Cook and Rachel Stevenson (eds.): <u>Bartlett Works - Architecture Buildings Projects</u>, August Projects / UCL, 2004 (p. 51)
[4] Peter Marcuse: <u>Walls of fear and walls of support</u> in Nan Ellin (ed.): <u>Architecture of Fear</u>, Princeton Architectural Press, 1997 (p. 104)

Wall as Interface - Wall as Skin

The meaning of walls, in general, is grounded in a long tradition in which they are considered boundaries and dividers of social, political and psychological domains. Walls can represent power, but also isolation; they can create security, but also fear. Walls have the power to eliminate the reality that fails to conform to it. When understood as skin they represent a defence system that safeguards our wholeness against the intrusion of dubious matter. It protects us from natural threats as well as our physical and moral integrity from the rest of humanity. To question the meaning of walls as a dividing boundary means to question the relationship between those who live on both sides of the wall. This is historically a troublesome relationship, which for long has been characterised by values of hierarchy, inequality, and domination[4] But, more than <u>Peter Marcuse</u>'s argument of an ideal society without walls and boundaries, it is far more challenging to consider a society in which <u>Inhabitable Interfaces</u> act as new means of social interaction - unifiers, rather than dividers; mechanisms of individual liberation, rather than of social imprisoning; interfaces with which we can interact and merge.

STUDY OF SITTING FACILITY BY WEN-TING CHAN DURING FENG CHIA & BARTLETT DIGITAL ARCHITECTURE WORKSHOP TAICHUNG TAIWAN · 2005

Mysterious and Haunted Walls – The Attraction for the Uncanny

The understanding of walls is the result of our early social
and spatial experiences, in particular, the ones related to the
hidden spaces of our houses. These potentially inhabitable
areas are like a repository of activities and memories since
our first childhood discoveries, which represent primal
shelters that raise primal fears; invisible and uncanny
spaces in hollow walls that we feel unconsciously attracted
to conquer and then occupy. Closets, attics, wall niches,
alcoves, storage cubicles, fire escapes, spaces underneath
staircases, backyard shelters, service chambers, basement
compartments and sheds embody a fascination in which
we project our fantasies and anxieties. These chambers are
spaces in which we are usually alone, isolated, or on the
way to somewhere else. Without them, one seems curiously
reduced to the present and somehow limited to the surface.
As Anne Troutman argues, "these curious places become the
refuge of the half-realised. Wishes, dreams, fantasies, fears,
desires are the inhabitants of the internal boundaries of our
everyday environment: the place of the other, the imagined,
the double, the dream."[5] Usually peripheral to the main
spaces, these spaces represent a potential attraction for their
marginal character, for their hidden uncanny, creating an
expanded boundary of the architecture and our experiential
unconsciousness.

The notion of both a real and projected life within these
secret spaces is intriguing for it suggests that the
architecture of Inhabitable Walls is an architecture that
assumes what Troutman considers 'double life' – one
simultaneously present through the open and visible
conditions, but also the enclosed and hidden spaces. It
is an architecture that makes out of this double life its
ultimate seduction. As she further suggests: "Consciously
and unconsciously, we assign meaning to every surface, every
cavity, visible and invisible until certain types of spaces
become associated with specific feelings and begin to form
pockets or sites for the contents of our inner lives.

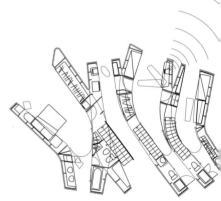

INHABITABLE WALLS OF LOFTING HOUSE
MARCOSANDMARJAN · 2005

From within these pockets we may occasionally glimpse our hopes and desires or sense our fears and anxieties."[6]

Inhabitable Interfaces are not to be confused with service cores, although they share to a certain extend a similar programme and attention when located in a building. Service cores are mainly defined functionally through the separation of secondary areas from the main spaces into a concentrated and efficient core. Inhabitable Interfaces, on the contrary, are defined conceptually and spatially, integrating part of the main programme of a building and usually acquiring a special meaning in the understanding of the whole building. These physical spaces are considered primordial and during the design stage clearly thought of as to integrate as many usually space-centred activities as possible. In these areas the human body encounters and physically touches the building. The wall literally becomes the interface between body and its surrounding, thus allowing not just a visual but also haptic experience of architecture.

In the research Hyperdermis done in 1999 and the latex models for Walls for Communicating People façades are proposed to incorporate data suits, sensor gloves and robotic prostheses that users wear to engage in virtual communication. The walls are highly networked, intelligent 'exoskeletal skins' that reflect Mitchell's visions in which the 'body net' will become linked to the 'building net', the 'building net' to the 'community net', and the 'community net' to the 'global net'. "From gesture sensors worn on our bodies to the world-wide infrastructure of communication satellites and long-distance fiber, the elements of the bitsphere will finally come together to form one densely interwoven system within which the knee bone is connected to the I-bahn."[7] For the user of Walls for Communicating People the three-dimensional digital interplay replaces the importance of the traditional computer screen by immersing the body simultaneously in the physical and virtual space. As a reflection of this, a combination of physical acts of

HYPERDERMIS
WALLS FOR COMMUNICATING PEOPLE
MARCOS CRUZ · LONDON · 1998-98
In the project Walls for Communicating People essential domestic functions such as sitting, sleeping or communicating are transferred from the traditional room-space into inhabitable appliance walls that incorporate several service-devices: Storage Capillaries, In-wall Seats, Relaxing Cocoons, Communication Suits and Gestural Tentacles. In this scenario people crawl into walls in order to sit, hang or lie in (hidden) chambers that are embedded within flexible and pliable surfaces. Here, walls are interfaces from which people can engage in virtual communication and be connected with the world-wide digital net. These actions that resemble acts of parasitic infiltration20, encompasse a new haptic

body penetration with that of a broadly virtual permeability becomes routine. The <u>Inhabitable Technologised Walls</u> of <u>Hyperdermis</u> are womb spaces <u>par excellence</u>, enclosed, but yet penetrable, anatomically ergonomic and protective.

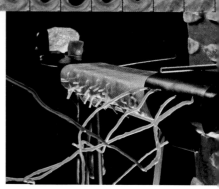

- -

[5] Anne Troutman: <u>Invisible Fear - Secret Places and Hidden Spaces in Dwellings</u> in Nan Ellin (ed.): <u>Architecture of Fear</u>, Princeton Architectural Press, 1997 (p. 145)
[6] Ibid. (p. 156)
[7] William J. Mitchell: <u>City of Bits - Space, Place and the Infobahn</u>, MIT Press, 1996 (p. 172/173)

PRELIMINARY SKETCH
OF HYPERDERMIS

relationship between the human body and a sensitive-reactive environment. Through these in-wall activities the movement of the outer façade reveals internal functions of the house. Like an urban 'corral reef', buildings with their exposed communication sleeves, tentacles and sitting bulges create an ever dynamic urban scenario.

<u>Storage Cappilaries</u>

The variable forms of Storage Capillaries have a simple storing procedure comparable to the fat storage in human skin. The building swells by storing the household paraphernalia in the walls. The outside membrane is made of a stretchable water-repellent material.21 In the inside a non-woven rubber composite is proposed for its pierce-resistant qualities, allowing the intrusion of sharp-edged objects into the storage spaces. Structurally, the stiffening of the embedded gel structure compensates for the weight of stored objects. But stability is also achieved by stretching the contents of the chambers under the surface under tension.

<u>In-wall Seats</u>

Proposed as a sitting facility like soft wall chairs, these devices take advantage of the extremely thin and flexible conditions of the wall. Similar to the three-layered construction of the storage capillaries, the wall is also responsive to weight and in this case to human movement. The inside

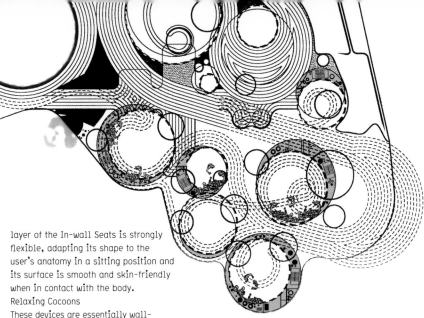

layer of the In-wall Seats is strongly
flexible, adapting its shape to the
user's anatomy in a sitting position and
its surface is smooth and skin-friendly
when in contact with the body.

Relaxing Cocoons

These devices are essentially wall-
incorporated bed facilities. These womb-
like enclosures are proposed as auto-
regenerating sleeping areas, in which an
artificial skin is implanted in the inner
membrane on a gel-embedded layer.

Communication Suits

The Suit is a computerised interface
for communication purposes. The user
dresses-up the wall, sliding into its
wearable wall sleeves. On the outside,
a microfibre textile membrane coats
the building. This is water-repellent
yet breathable for sweating bodies in
communication action. The structural
layer changes its rigidity according
to electromagnetic data inputs and
also adapts its internal stability to
physical body behaviour during the
communication process. Just like the
relaxing cocoon, artificial skin is
implanted in the inner membrane on
a gel-embedded layer. The artificial
hairy skin is touch sensitive, being
colonised by microscopic optical fibres
and embedded in ink-resistive flexible
sensors. For visual input a soft helmet
with a double liquid screen has been
included, which also incorporates
stereoscopic effects in the suit.

INHABITABLE WALLS IN EXHIBITION CONES
DETAIL PLAN OF COMPETITION PROPOSAL FOR THE NEW
TOMIHIRO MUSEUM · MARCOSANDMARJAN · 2002

These electronic organs interface
with the body's sensory receptors and
muscles, receiving and sending data
signals from and to a central processor.

Gestural Tentacles

The Gestural Tentacles protect the users
inside from external vicissitudes that
might disturb their behaviour. Like
insect antennas, these extremities
are hyper sensitive to touch and are
equipped with teleceptors through which
exterior action can be detected and
whose effect can be turned down

Figural Ornaments as Wall Inhabitants

But is the phenomenon of inhabiting walls so new?

The presence of bodies in walls and façades has a long
history, in particular since the Renaissance where the
human body acquires a fundamental importance. In her
essay on figural ornaments Alina Payne[8] lists numerous
types of human figures that form part of an extensive
repertoire of figural ornaments, which were traditionally
associated with a religious type, and then brought into
the realm of the profane. We witnessed in this period a
growing sculpturalisation of architecture in which figures
are employed to enhance the formal and tectonic expression
of buildings. For Payne, the figural ornament thus augments
the combination between structural and corporeal references,
transforming the tactile richness of architecture through
textures, light, shades, and movement in elements of the
façade into an increasingly integrated wall corporeality.[9]
Figures suddenly start inhabiting walls and façades in which
"the architectural details belong to sculpture in the same way
that the geometry of the bodies placed along pyramids and
diagonals suggests that they belong to architecture."[10] Hence,
the Renaissance sees the transition of figural ornaments from
a sculptural motif to an architectural one. Figures cease
being exceptional object to be walked around and become
one of many that anonymously 'inhabit' the architecture.
The Baroque then introduces many more figures into the
wall wishing for an unprecedented ornamental richness of
sensuous attraction. This is particularly noticeable in the
eighteenth century Portuguese Baroque and the majestic inner
décor of churches entitled as Talha Dourada, where the work
of Miguel Francisco da Silva stands out for high exuberance
and splendour.
Less cheerful, but more rooted in the tectonic of the building
can be listed the work of German and Austrian architects
such as Johann Lukas von Hildebrandt, Johann Bernhard
Fischer von Erlach and Johann Balthasar Neumann. But it is

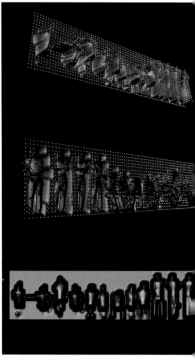

FLL FOLLIES · MARCOSANDMARJAN · 2005

the sense of fantasy and humour that is mostly represented in <u>Wendel Dietterlin's</u> (1550-1599) drawings. "Human figures, threatening demons, exotic creatures, and mythological beasts become extensions of the architecture, peering out from its darker lithic niches, indeed sometimes tearing at its very fabric."[11]

Hence, the phenomenon of figural ornamentation suggests that in certain periods of our history (in particular in the Baroque and Rococo period) the aspiration to fill and 'inhabit' walls was of fundamental importance. The merge of <u>Human Flesh</u> within the <u>Architectural Flesh</u> was celebrated and accomplished in an unparalleled 'theatricalisation' of architecture. Here, as never before, the aristocratic indulgence in spectacle, tactility, and sensual richness of ornament resulted in this exploitation of appearance.

But from the eighteenth century onwards the exposure of bodies was to be dramatically erased from architecture. A historic process of aesthetic and moral change was about to unfold that cleaned the wall from its ornament and increasingly disembodied architecture. With an unprecedented anti-flesh Puritanism that reached far into the twentieth century, public and domestic inhabitation routines were to become obliterated from architecture.

- -

[8] Alina Payne: <u>Reclining bodies: Figural Ornament in Renaissance Architecture</u> in George Dodds; Robert Tavernor (ed.): <u>Body and Building - Essays on the Changing Relation of Body and Architecture</u>, The MIT Press 2002 (p. 94-113)
[9] Ibid. (p. 108)
[10] Ibid. (p. 109)
[11] Harry Francis Mallgrave: <u>Dancing wih Vitruvius: Corporeal Fantasies in Nothern Classicism</u> in George Dodds; Robert Tavernor (ed.): <u>Body and Building - Essays on the Changing Relation of Body and Architecture</u>, The MIT Press 2002 (p. 131)

<u>Bourgeois detachment - seeking for privacy, cleanliness and social order</u>

To understand this phenomenon of bodily detachment it is necessary to make an incursion into the historical development of housing typologies. According to <u>Robin Evans</u> in probably all domestic spaces until the middle of the seventeenth century, there is no distinction between the circulation through the house and the complex system of thoroughly interconnected chambers within. Rooms have numerous doors that are placed in the most convenient way in order to lead us to as many parts of the building as possible. Evans observes here an inversion of the meaning of convenience. In the sixteenth century a convenient room was one, which had many doors, however later in the nineteenth century it is a room that has just one door.

This is due to the emergence of the bourgeoisie in the late eighteenth and nineteenth century, which begins to seek for increasing privacy within the domestic scene, pursuing preservation of the self, and independence and separation form others. This results in an increasing demarcation and differentiation of spaces inside the house. Social and individual requirements drive parts of the dwelling to be separated systematically into two independently functioning spheres: an unoccupied circulation network for 'serving', and an inner succession of gradually more disconnected private rooms for the 'served'. A typical case of such typological arrangement is visible in Lluís Domènech I Montaner's Casa Fuster, built in Barcelona between 1908 and 1911, where the reminiscent heritage of a palazzo-type organisation into a four-story high urban apartment block. Here, the rather classical but extreme variety of individual spaces enhances the singularity of interconnecting rooms. It is an sophisticated typological example, in which a distinction between the upper and lower ranks of the house is marked by the parallel use of isolated closets, interconnecting rooms sustaining direct sequential circulation for the privileged, at the same time allocating servants to specific adjacent confinements. The circulation, which is characterised by a mixed use of corridors and interconnected rooms - in some cases the aligned location of doors form an implicit corridor area inside the room spaces, and service spaces are separated from the main domain of the bourgeois family life. But Casa Fuster is not

CASA FUSTER
LLUÍS DOMÈNECH I MONTANER ·
BARCELONA, 1908-11
The 'in-wall services' of Lluís Domènech I Montaner's Casa Fuster are a series of bath and toilet cubicles ingeniously located in between each contiguous bedroom along the inner side of the representative façades of the building. Domènech inverts the common location of such services normally in less exposed inner areas of the house by locating the most intimate sphere of this early twentieth century upper class family on the outmost edge of its private life. As an in-between area between outside and inside, these internal wall protrusions narrow down the access from the rooms to the balcony dramatising the proximity to the street life and conferring them, from an inner perspective, with more spatial depth. The narrowing-down effect creates a protective filter for excessive insulation and privacy in particular - a shield against any invasive gaze from the outside.

DETAIL PLAN OF SOUTH FAÇADE WITH IN-WALL CLOSETS AND BATHS

just paradigmatic in its spatial organisation, but even more intriguing for the ingenious location of intimate service areas - baths and toilets - in the external walls of the building. As the result of a new typological evolution in which each great bourgeois urban house integrated separate spaces dedicated to private hygiene in annexe to the bedrooms, the traditionally small washbasins or bathing containers in the bedrooms are transformed into tiny and completely enclosed spaces within the walls in which no more than one person should enter.

Adolf Loos's houses represent other interesting examples in which spatial and social segregation, as well as individual protectionism is combined with a high level of bodily experience of space. In his Moller House, built in Vienna between 1928 and 1929, a complex and refined corridor-based bourgeois-housing typology is related with a highly sophisticated arrangement of internal visual control. By positioning the lady's room on a raised alcove protruding from the street façade, the bourgeois occupant can oversee the goings-on inside the house, while simultaneously being able to screen activities on the street from behind a curtain. Beatriz Colomina's brilliant analysis of the house and its internal voyeuristic subtleties gives us a clear idea of these refined systems of control in and outside the private domain.[12] But Loos' understanding of architecture is based even on a different premise, as she well recognises. "Loos privileges the bodily experience of space over its mental construction: the architect first senses the space, then he visualises it."[13] He establishes an alternative strategy in which corporeal inhabitation and tactile wall-related experience of space are developed in parallel with a stylistic 'purification' of architecture against the excesses of old-style decoration. The lady's room represents an inhabitation routine with an intrinsically sensual 'wallism'. It can be considered a 'womb-like' space in which the occupants literally sit in the wall seeking comfort that is more than just sensual, for there it is also a spatial-psychological

MOLLER HOUSE
ADOLF LOOS · VIENNA · 1928-29

The 'lady's room' in Adolf Loos' Moller House is an inhabitable wall-niche located at the periphery of the house, protruding as a raised volume extending from the main street façade, just above the main entrance. What is interesting about this 'in-wall sitting' is its voyeuristic location, rather than its typological order. As Beatriz Colomina thoroughly describes, the lady of the house is literally sitting in between the outside and inside sphere, and through the window she can easily detect anyone crossing the outer threshold of the house. She is in a position of highest security from which she can scrutinise and overview the main activities happening outside as well as inside the house. Her gaze can pierce cross diagonally through the darkness of the circulation and living room areas and reach the garden in the back. At the same time, she is able to intercept anyone who ascends the staircases from the entrance and for whom she is shielded by the backlight of the area she sits in.

DETAIL SECTION WITH LADY'S ROOM AND IN-WALL SITTING FACILITY

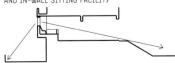

aspect to this higher and in-between sitting that can be read in terms of a regime of power and control of the frightened upper class exerted upon the lower class that works both inside and outside the house.

- -

[12] Beatriz Colomina: The Split Wall - Domestic Voyeurism in Beatriz Colomina (ed.): Sexuality & Space, Princeton Papers on Architecture, Princeton Architectural Press, 1992 (p. 72-128)
[13] Ibid. (p. 91)

Becoming Networked

Meanwhile, another important phenomenon that affects architecture throughout the end of nineteenth century and early twentieth century becomes crucial for the understanding of Inhabitable Interfaces, i.e. the emergence of the technologised wall. While the pre-industrial urban house is a disconnected entity from any kind of physical network, it is technically limited to large structural walls, which host a lot of smaller ancillary spaces, such as staircases, cupboards, fireplaces, bed cupboards, latrines, window seats, etc. The modern technologised house, on the contrary, is determined by a substantial reduction of wall thickness and the detachment of walls from the structure, replacing the wall-incorporated chambers by a new mechanical apparatus of ducts and appliances in the walls. In a first step the house and its internal functions become connected to a larger urban network of systems in which water, gas, electricity (and later telephone and television) results in a total reconstruction of the world above and below the cities. Few examples illustrate this in such an ostentatious manner as Pierre Charreau's Maison de Verre, built in Paris between 1927 and 1928. Typical for an early twentieth century bourgeois family, the modern kitchen and sanitary facilities are available in large quantities to regulate and maintain the functional proprieties and hygiene of a 'civilised modern body'. Its exuberant design of appliances and utensils replace the traditional servants that assisted the family in preparing food or in their personal cleaning rituals. The Maison de Verre presents us with two types of Inhabitable Wall Interfaces: wall-embedded

Maison de Verre
Pierre Charreau · Paris, 1927-28
In Pierre Charreau's Maison de Verre the use of the sanitary and clinical equipment represents a different type of inhabitation that is intrinsically wall-dependent and connected to the wider urban supply network. As body prosthetics, the equipment is designed ergonomically to fit the body, which in standing, sitting or lying position becomes linked to the wall as if with a new umbilical cord -supplying water, electricity and able to discharge its waste. The feeling of being networked is also manifested by deliberately exposing the fittings, ducts and connecting pipes, which are detached from floors and walls following a twentieth century trend towards absolute hygiene inside one of the most polluting part of the house. The amount of toilets and washing areas that are placed all over the house, as much as the light being reflected on the polished surfaces of metal and ceramic materials is here not just a demonstration of a clean aesthetic, but rather based on a clinical aesthetic of sanitary outfits, which can also be found in the doctor's equipment on the ground floor.

services in one of the remaining party walls and the washing cabinets in the dormitories. The inhabited niches of the party wall are reminiscent of walls of pre-industrial houses. Each cavity seems to be used for a different functional purpose varying in size and closure. They hide the dirtiest functions of the house, such as toilets, washing areas for clothes, storage, waste, etc. The washing cabinets, on the other hand, are conspicuously exposed in a modernist gesture that displays technology and modern hygiene as a symbol of social sophistication and beauty. The raised closet and new devices become showpieces that can be secluded behind moveable translucent screens exhibiting the washing rituals in an intimate theatrical manner.

Later, in many projects of the ninety sixty's and seventy's the fascination with intelligent skins and technologised walls gets to such degree that they are treated as a sort of fetish. This is for example notorious in the involvement and love relationship between people and their physical surrounding in Roger Vadim's movie Barbarella, or in the hand-carvable-space-frame principle[14] that Christopher Alexander's proposes for five feet deep walls that can be changed and adapted deliberately to the users wishes. In that period Reyner Banham, for example, realises that all the new appliances and technical networks could represent half or even more of the total cost of a house at that time. By questioning the traditional understanding of a building when incorporating such a degree of "piping, flues, ducts, wires, lights, outlets, ovens, sinks, refuse disposers, hi-fi reverberators, antennae, conduits, freezers, heaters"[15], he proposes that this hardware could eventually stand up by itself without the constructive shell of the traditional house. His article is accompanied by François Dallegret's proposal of an Anatomy of a Dwelling, which radically epitomises the literal reduction of the house to its domestic gadgetry. It can be seen as the house of a contemporary networked body in its pre-computerised stage. The networking of buildings and walls is yet to be challenged by further developments. With new developments

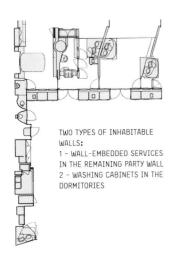

TWO TYPES OF INHABITABLE WALLS:
1 - WALL-EMBEDDED SERVICES IN THE REMAINING PARTY WALL
2 - WASHING CABINETS IN THE DORMITORIES

in the digital realm of the information era our buildings start
to become connected to a world-wide electronic network.
Here, telecommunication systems are replacing conventional
circulation systems, and the solvent of digital information
is potentially decomposing traditional building types.
William Mitchell says: "As the speed at which bits zip around
a building approaches that at which they are moved inside
today's computers, as different sorts of specialised sensors
and input devices harvest bits at arbitrary locations, as
processors are embedded wherever they happen to be needed,
and as all the various displays and appliances are integrated
into building-wide, digitally controlled systems, it becomes
meaningless to ask where the smart electronics end and the
dumb construction begins; computers are bursting out of their
boxes, walls are becoming wired and the architectural works
of the bit-sphere less structured with chips than robots with
foundations."[16]
But Mitchell points out, here, that clothes have traditionally
shaped our first interface with the physical world as much as
our personal electronic devices or intelligent clothes are now
creating interfaces between our nervous system and the world-
wide digital net. Such ideas are preceded by Mike Webb's
Cushicle project, done in 1966, where a house is reduced to a
deployable and portable suit. The suit is fitted-out with high-
tech equipment, which the user carries around on their back.
When needed the user can inflate the peumatic body suit,
which pops open into a cocoon like space into which the user
can slide. Similar to the later project Suitaloon, completed
in 1967, the Cushicle is thought as a comfortable and fully-
served mechanism in which the distinctions between body,
clothing, media, and shelter are blurred, enabling the user to
satisfy their needs unimpeded by the material restrictions of
traditional architecture.

- -
[14] "Most of the identity of a dwelling lies in or near its surfaces - in the three of four feet
near the walls, floors and ceilings. This is where people keep most of their belongings, this
is where special lighting fixtures are, this is where special built-in furniture is placed, this
is where the special cosy nooks and corners are that individual family members make their
own." But he recognises that "Present construction makes this virtually impossible. Walls,
floors, ceilings are hard, brittle and thin. They are hard to work, most modifications require

Cushicle (Deployable Suit)
Mike Webb • 1966

With the establishment of service nodes
and additional optional apparatus
in the city, Mike Webb's autonomous
Cushicle is thought to be an inhabitable
parasite that can be plugged-in
temporarily into the city to become part
of a more widespread urban network of
personalised enclosures. Its integrated
metallic skeleton - spinal system - can
transform according to walking, sitting,
relaxing and resting needs forming the
chassis for the incorporated high-tech
appliances. It contains food, water
supply, radio, a miniature projection
television and a heating apparatus.
The radio and TV are contained in
the helmet and the food and water
supply are carried in pod attachments.
The other major component of the
deployable suit is the inclusion of
extra skins as viewing screens, which
controls the atmosphere within. Both
systems open out consecutively or can
be used independently. Various models
of Cushicle envelope and suit were
thought to be available ranging from
super sports to family models.
The Inhabitable Suit is aimed at a
technologicalised and consumerist
society, in which the modern nomad,
a bourgeois descendent now turned
into urban middle-class explorer, a
'wanderer' or telecommuter, becomes
part of the global phenomenon of
ultimate mobility and bio-mechanical
freedom.

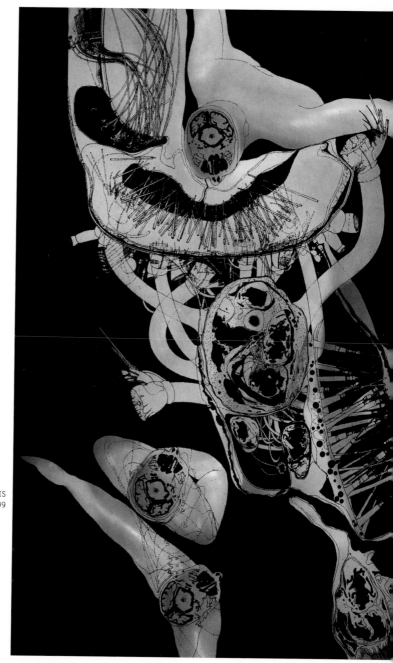

HYPERDERMIS
MARCOS CRUZ · LONDON · 1998/99

CUSHICLE
MIKE WEBB · 1966

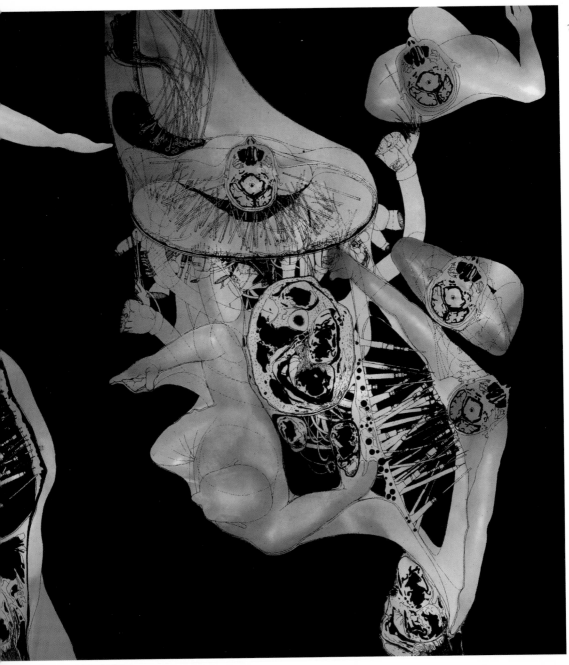

structural alterations and the finish is of such kind that local changes always look tacked on and amateurish. (...) In order to give these walls the two characteristics defined above, they must be made of some material which is inherently structural - so that however much of it gets carved out, the whole remains rigid and the surface remains continuous no matter how much is removed or added, it requires only point or paper or cloth covering to finish it. We may visualize such a material most easily by thianking of the internal structure of a bone - which is a kind of micro-space frame. We may carve our any amount of it - the rest still stands. This is the intention of hand-carvable-space-frame, as defined in the pattern. (...) These walls must be extremely deep. To contain shelves, cabinets, deisplays, special lights, special surfaces, deep reveal windows, individual niches, built in seats and nooks, the walls must be at least three feet deep; if possible five feet deep." Christopher Alexander: <u>Thick Wall Pattern</u> in Architectural Design, June 1967

[15] Reyner Banham: <u>A home is not a house</u> in AD 1/69 (p. 45)
[16] William J. Mitchell: <u>City of Bits - Space, Place and the Infobahn</u>, MIT Press, 1996 (p. 171)

Dressing Walls

<u>Webbs'</u> architectural dressing can be understood as a technologised reinvention of <u>Gottfried Semper's</u> and <u>Adolf Loos'</u> belief that a buildings should be worn rather than merely occupied is revived. <u>Semper's</u> <u>Principle of Dressing</u> (Prinzip der Bekleidung) and <u>Loos'</u> <u>Law of Dressing</u> (Gesetz der Bekleidung) both favoured a continuous "sensory play" of smell, sound and tactile experience through "the folds, twists, and turns in an often discontinuous ornamental surface."[17] For <u>Beatriz Colomina</u>, <u>Adolf Loos'</u> architecture represents a form of covering in which not walls are covered, but the occupants are enveloped and wrapped in the building as with clothes, as it is seen in the décor of his wife's bedroom.[18] It is a conceptual play between 'architectural dressing' and 'bodily dressing', which places the body literally within the 'fabric' of architecture. This is clearly stated in what <u>Josep Quetglas'</u> describes as 'architecture of the placenta' (arquitectura de la placenta). For <u>Guetglas</u>, who was <u>Colomina's</u> former teacher, <u>Adolf Loos</u> "wants to rebuild, regain that unique peaceful and consolatory environment of the maternal refuge."[19] <u>Quetglas'</u> argument suggests that the phenomenon of wall inhabitation echoes an innate desire for the lost primary shelter of the mother - the womb and the anxieties of the exit from it. Therefore the architectural 'dressing' (Bekleidung) can be seen as an attempt to recover the lost protection of the womb. In other words, to dress architecture is to experience it through touch and thus rely on an innate and ultimate

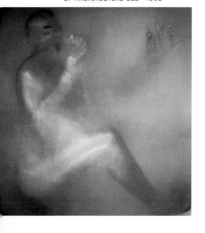

HYPERDERMIS - PERFORMANCE IN LATEX WALL AT THE BARTLETT SCHOOL OF ARCHITECTURE UCL · 1998

psychological condition in which we endeavour to transgress the boundaries of our bodies within the boundaries of the architecture's inner flesh.

A project that features several of the previously analysed inhabitable wall interfaces is tested in the proposal for the New Godet Club in Istanbul, done by marcosandmarjan in 2003. Here the mobile DJ-capsule works as a call-the-attention street icon that disappears in the façade when there is no interior activity and stretching out when the club flourishes at night. The DJ-capsule is like stretchable façade-suit in which the DJ is sitting, and from which the bar level and especially the dance floor are clearly seen. It shares a strategic location within the building as the lady's room in Loos' Moller house, while reinterpreting the temporary expansion of Webb's Cushicle. It is the highest point in the whole bar – a connected and networked chamber that shines in the exterior darkness of the night and disappears in contra-light in the heights of the noisy and uproarious interior. It is a podium that seems untouchable, a sanctorum from where the DJ co-ordinates the music and the majority of the inner media activities. From the outside it is an exposed and rather vulnerable place. As the inhabitants of the communication suits in Hyperdermis, the DJ is here a wall creature that turns the whole façade into an inhabitable, malleable and dynamic interface that reveals to the exterior the internal activities of the club.

Parallel to this can be found a series of other twentieth century projects where the concept of wall inhabitation is applied as a primary design strategy for buildings of a larger scale. Different from the predominantly housing typology, these projects integrate inner and outer Inhabitable Wall Interfaces, Inhabitable Cones, Columns, etc. It therefore follows a comparative analysis to understand better the different design strategies behind these projects.

(cont. p. 84)

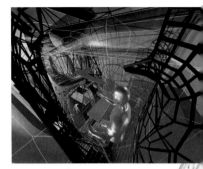

New Godet Club
marcosandmarjan · 2003

Located in the Beyoglu district of Istanbul, an area with predominantly European-style nineteenth century housing and the centre for entertainment and nightlife, the club was proposed to be situated just off the main shopping street of Istanbul announcing itself through the protrusion of the DJ-capsule on the street façade. It was proposed as a new centre for innovative and experimental multi-media activities in the city. The programmatic organisation of the club into differentiated acoustic areas triggers the concept of a 'Floating Vessel', an enclosed chill-out lounge hovering over the noisy open areas of entrance, bar and dance floors. The construction of the capsule and the vessel shows an 'Inlucent' materiality: a translucent resin membrane that incorporates a metallic skeleton with technical appliances, robotic devices, and audio-visual equipment, exposing itself as the visible 'vascular system' of the club. In the entrance floor, pressure-sensitive resin cushions change the luminosity and colour saturation according to the

[17] Mark Wigley: <u>White Walls, Designer Dresses – The Fashioning of Modern Architecture</u>, The MIT Press, 1995 (p.11)
[18] Beatriz Colomina: <u>The Split Wall – Domestic Voyeurism</u> in Beatriz Colomina (ed.): <u>Sexuality & Space</u>, Princeton Papers on Architecture, Princeton Architectural Press, 1992 (p. 92)
[19] Josep Quetglas: <u>Lo Placentero</u> in Passsado a Limpio I (p. 60), originally published in Carrer de la Ciutat n.9 & 10, January 1980 (p. 2)

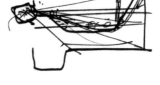

PRELIMINARY SKETCHES
SECTION STUDY WITH STRATEGIC
LOCATION OF DJ-CAPSULE

variable space occupation. On the dance floor, flexible flat screens are sound-responsive and linked to the Internet. On the walls, a series of monitor vessels react to the air quality creating an ever-changeable pattern of biological matter.[2]

STREET FACADE
WITH PROTRUSION
DJ-CAPSULE

Sleeping Vessel

Inlucency of Soft Perception, Competition proposal
for the Headquarters of New England Biolabs,
Massachusetts USA, 2001

WIREMESH MODEL OF LAB CONES AND ROOF

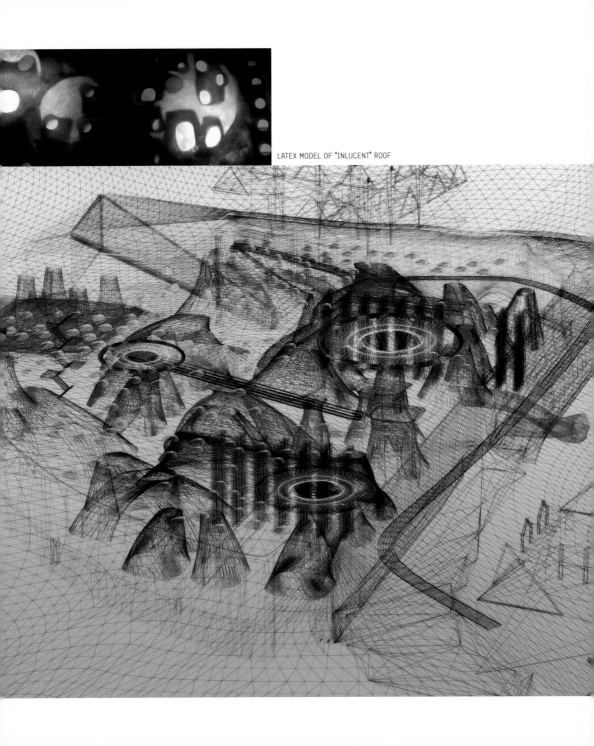

LATEX MODEL OF "INLUCENT" ROOF

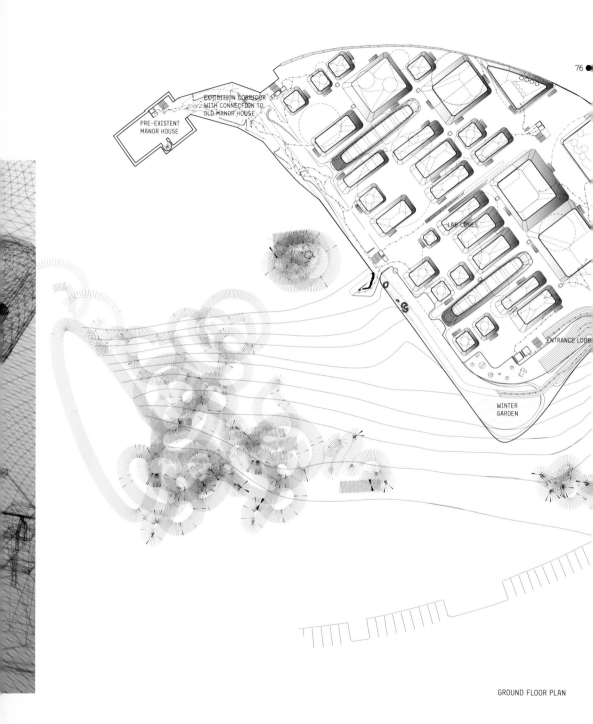

PRE-EXISTENT
MANOR HOUSE

EXHIBITION CORRIDOR
WITH CONNECTION TO
OLD MANOR HOUSE

LAB CONES

ENTRANCE LOBB

WINTER
GARDEN

GROUND FLOOR PLAN

TEAM » DESIGN: MARCOSANDMARJAN › COLLABORATORS: SHAO MING, HUI HUI TEOH,
SHIE-WEI PAN › BIOLOGY CONSULTANT: ORLANDO DE JESUS › STRUCTURAL ENGINEERING: DANIEL
BOSIA - OVE ARUP AND PARTNERS
PROGRAMME » 280 SCIENTIFIC WORK AREAS: 9300 M^2 › WET LAB AREA, SCIENTISTS OFFICE AREA,
LAB SUPPORT SPACES, MECHANICAL SPACES, CENTRAL DISHWARE-MEDIA PREPARATION AREA: 420
M^2 › FERMENTATION LABORATORIES: 450 M^2 › SHIPPING AREA AND PACKAGING EQUIPMENT: 1150 M^2
› LECTURE ROOM: 350 M^2 › FACILITIES DEPARTMENT, OFFICES, SHOP, STORAGE: 450 M^2 › WINTER-
GARDEN FOR TROPICAL PLANTS: 1000 M^2
› MAIN CORRIDORS, STAIRS, ELEVATOR, MECH. TOILETS, EMPLOYEE LOUNGES: 1000 M^2 › PARKING
AREA: 180 CARS › TOTAL NEW BUILDING AREA: 14120 M^2

- -

THE NEW NEB HEADQUARTERS PRESENT ITSELF AS A CLINICAL VESSEL THAT STRETCHES OUT A
MASSIVE SURFACE FROM THE FEET OF THE MAIN MANSION ON THE SITE. THE BUILDING SUBMERGES
ITS IMMENSE VOLUME INTO THE TOPOGRAPHY, LETTING ITS INHABITABLE ROOF (DIS)APPEAR AS A
DEEP-DIMENSIONAL SCREEN. THE WINTER GARDEN SURROUNDS THE INTERIOR LAB AREAS WITH A
DOUBLE LAYERED TRANSPARENT MEMBRANE CREATING AN ENIGMATIC (RATHER INTRIGUING) GREEN
FAÇADE THAT INVITES TO ENGAGEMENT AND INVESTIGATION. WHILE THE MANUFACTURE-LABO-
RATORIES ARE HIDDEN UNDERNEATH THE EARTH, THE LOCATION OF THE OFFICES ALLOWS EACH
SCIENTIST TO SIT IN THE ROOF IN TINY CAPSULES THAT 'TOUCH THE BIG SKY'.
THE TABLE CONCEPT
THE IDEA OF A TABLE SUGGESTS THAT THE INTERNAL DISTRIBUTION IS ORGANISED IN ROOF,
CONES, AND IN-BETWEEN SPACES. THE ROOF EMBEDS ALL OFFICE AREAS FOR SCIENTISTS TO
CONTEMPLATE THE SURROUNDING LANDSCAPE. UNDERNEATH, THE LAB-CONES FUNCTION AS THE
STRUCTURAL SKELETON INTEGRATING LABORATORY SPACES OF VARIABLE SIZE. THE RESULTING
IN-BETWEEN SPACES ARE USED FOR CIRCULATION AREAS, RESTING ZONES AND DIVERSE SUPPORT
EQUIPMENT. THE 'INLUCENT' RESIN MASS PLAYS HOST TO ALL MAJOR APPLIANCES AND BLURS VARI-
ABLE INTENSITIES OF LIGHT TO THE ENCLOSED LAB AREAS UNDERNEATH. THE RESIN SURFACE, AND
A VARIETY OF INCORPORATED PHOTO-CHROMATIC CHEMICALS PROVOKE A 'SOFT PERCEPTION' OF
SPACE. PERFORMANCE SPECIFICATION OF THE SKIN VARIES CONTINUOUSLY FROM PROPERTIES OF A
RIGID STRUCTURE, OPAQUE SURFACE TO THOSE OF A FLEXIBLE, TRANSPARENT MEMBRANE.

AUDITORIUM

PRE-EXISTENT MANOR HOUSE

AERIAL VIEW OF LABORATORIES
AND PRE-EXISTENT MANOR HOUSES

RENDERING OF TWO-AND-A-HALF
DIMENSIONALITY

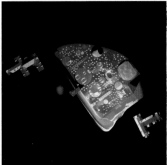

Garden of Vessels

Competition proposal for the New Tomihiro Museum,
Azuma Village Japan, 2002

GENERAL VIEW FROM UNDERNEATH

CONCEPT OF A BAGPIPE

CLAY MODEL OF EXHIBITION CONES

CIRCULATION

LATEX MODEL OF EXHIBITION CONES AND 'INLUCENT' ROOF

ORNAMENTAL PATTERN
OF FIRST FLOOR PLAN

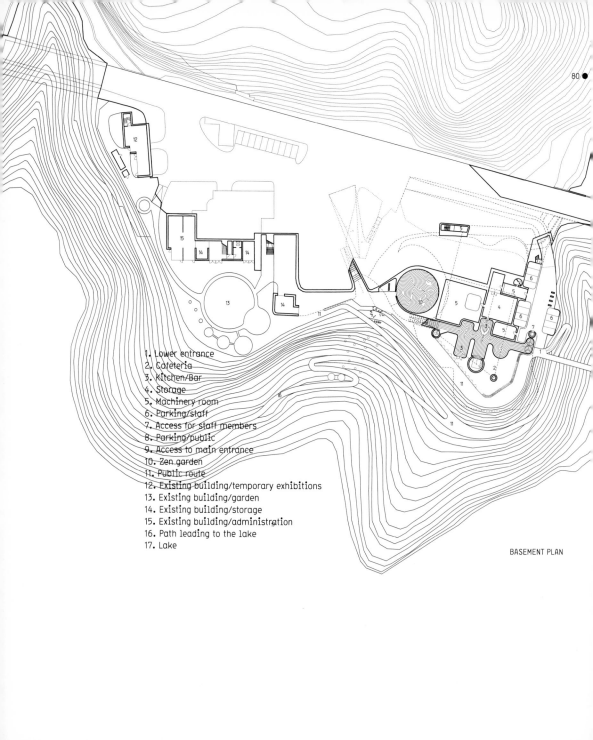

1. Lower entrance
2. Cafeteria
3. Kitchen/Bar
4. Storage
5. Machinery room
6. Parking/staff
7. Access for staff members
8. Parking/public
9. Access to main entrance
10. Zen garden
11. Public route
12. Existing building/temporary exhibitions
13. Existing building/garden
14. Existing building/storage
15. Existing building/administration
16. Path leading to the lake
17. Lake

BASEMENT PLAN

1. Main entrance
2. Water surface
3. Waterfall
4. Islands/workstations
5. Temporary exhibitions/projection spaces/multimedia
6. Access to exhibition cones
7. Service entrance/docking bay/goods lift
8. Panoramic deck/exterior performance platform
9. Existing building/administration
10. Existing building/temporary exhibitions
11. Parking/staff
12. Parking/public

GROUND FLOOR PLAN

AERIAL VIEW

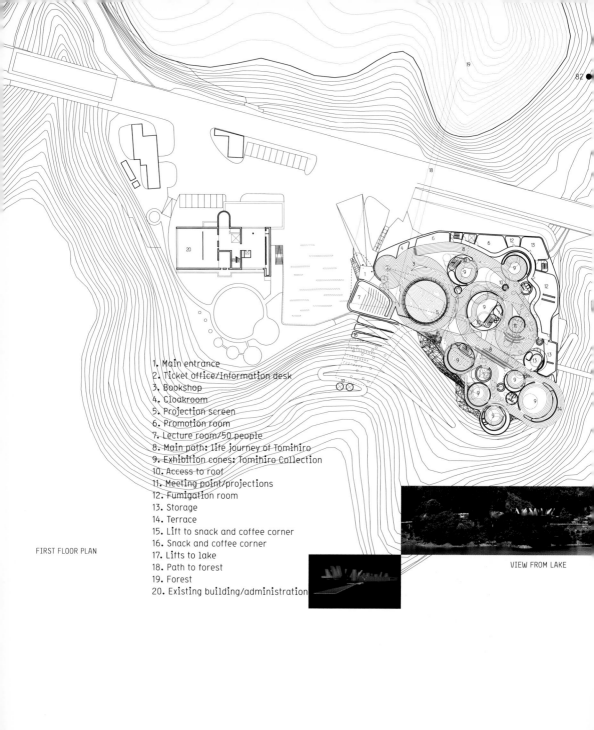

FIRST FLOOR PLAN

1. Main entrance
2. Ticket office/Information desk
3. Bookshop
4. Cloakroom
5. Projection screen
6. Promotion room
7. Lecture room/50 people
8. Main path: life journey of Tomihiro
9. Exhibition cones: Tomihiro Collection
10. Access to roof
11. Meeting point/projections
12. Fumigation room
13. Storage
14. Terrace
15. Lift to snack and coffee corner
16. Snack and coffee corner
17. Lifts to lake
18. Path to forest
19. Forest
20. Existing building/administration

VIEW FROM LAKE

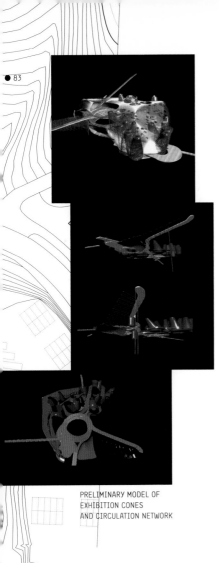

PRELIMINARY MODEL OF
EXHIBITION CONES
AND CIRCULATION NETWORK

Team » Design: marcosandmarjan › Collaborator: Andres Aguilar, Steve Pike, Jens Ritter, Hui Hui Teoh, Wanda Yu-Ying Hu › Planned site » Site area: 65000 m² › Leased: 5000 m² » Programme » Construction costs and exterior construction: 1.2 billion yen › Number of works to be displayed: 130 Parking places › Number of visitors annually 400000 › Permanent collection rooms: 900 m² › Planned exhibition room: 120 m² › Storage rooms: 330 m² › Stock room: 100 m² › Other: lecture room for 50 people, meeting space, bookshop, promotion room, snack and coffee corner, performances corner, fumigation rooms › Total new building area: 3000 m²

- -

To visit the New Tomihiro Museum of SHI-GA is to enter a reinterpreted landscape. The meandering route presents a process of discovery, a metaphorical life journey of Tomihiro himself. Passing through, and between, numerous and varying exhibition vessels, the experience is one of incidences of confluence and activity interspersed with moments of contemplation and intimacy. Travelling along suspended paths the sensation of floating – parallel to artworks 'floating' against their neutral landscape - is communicated. Continuing beyond the physical boundaries of the Museum, specific paths provide connections to the forest above and the lake below. The possibility of a real encounter with surrounding nature is raised. An internalised garden, separating the exhibition spaces from the rest of the Museum, allows for visual awareness of seasonal change; rain, snow, and blossom falling 'within' the museum.

The external envelope coalesces these elements. Transparent and occasionally translucent, it is interrupted by the liberal intrusion of light cones. Laminated timber provides the primary structure. The exhibition vessels consist of a dual layered skin, services and other ancillary requirements existing in the space between. An opaque internal layer affords deliberate control of light and humidity, necessary to the environment in which Tomihiro's work is presented. The existing museum is to be maintained as a venue for a rotating programme of temporary exhibitions. A new external communal space is created between it and the new Museum, promoting social activity.

The New Tomihiro Museum of SHI-GA brings together communal interaction and private introspection. The actual and metaphorical assembly of water, forest, stones and bridges combine to create a reinterpreted landscape in which to experience the work of Tomihiro

INHABITABLE INTERFACES - COMPARATIVE ANALYSIS

Entrance, Structure
Filtered natural light
Confessionals, Chapels
Circulation,
Conceptual: Modulor,
Virgin Mary

NOTRE-DAME DU HAUT
LE CORBUSIER
RONCHAMP, 1950-55

- - - - - - - - - - - - - -

Church

Partial circulation with view
points, Structure, Exhibition
surface

ASGER JORN MUSEUM (PROPOSAL)
JORN UTZON
SILKEBORG, 1963

- - - - - - - - - - - - - -

Museum

Entrance, Structure
Light, Appliance Walls
Toilets/Closets, Storage

THE HOUSE OF THE FUTURE
ALISON AND PETER SMITHSON
LONDON, 1955-56

- - - - - - - - - - - - - -

House

Entrance, Structure, Filtered
natural light, Technical Equipment, Toilets, Ventilation,
Ancillary spaces

SAINSBURY CENTRE FOR VISUAL
ARTS
NORMAN FOSTER
NORWICH, 1978

- - - - - - - - - - - - - -

Museum and Art School

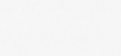
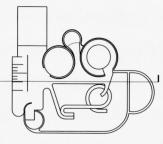
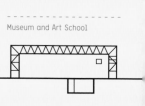
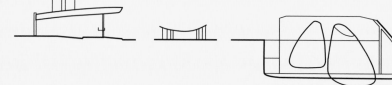

INHABITABLE INTERFACES - COMPARATIVE ANALYSIS

Circulation, Structure, Filtered
natural light, Technical Equipment, Toilets Ventilation, Ancillary spaces, Billboard area

CENTRE GEORGE POMPIDOU
RICHARD ROGERS / RENZO PIANO
PARIS, 1971-77

- - - - - - - - - - - - - -
Museum

Entrance, Ticket Office, Structure,
Artificial light, Technical Equipment, Ventilation, Ancillary
spaces, Service Lifts

KUNSTHAAL
REM KOOLHAAS / OMA
ROTTERDAM, 1988-92

- - - - - - - - - - - - -
Art Centre

Circulation, Structure, Artificial
light, Technical Equipment, Ventilation, Service Lifts, Conceptual:
Neutrons

MEDIATHEQUE
TOYO ITO
SENDAI, 1997-2001

- - - - - - - - - - - -
Mediatheque

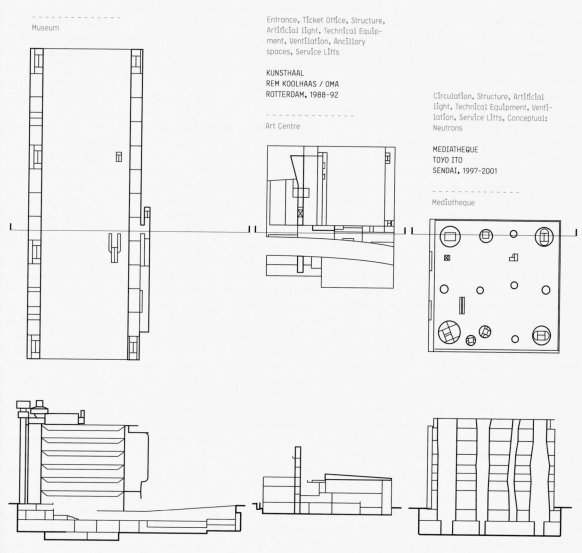

INHABITABLE INTERFACES - COMPARATIVE ANALYSIS

Mediatheque, Media Cells, Structure, Natural and Artificial light from skylights,
Bix - Media façade, Technical Equipment,
Toilets, Ventilation, Entrance from
underneath, Ancillary Spaces, Storage

KUNSTHAUS GRAZ
SPACELAB UK - PETER COOK / COLIN
FOURNIER
GRAZ, 2000-2003

- -
Art Centre

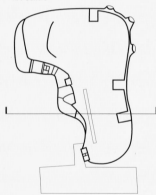

Entrances, Media cells, Structure
Filtered natural light through "inlucent" sili-
cone membrane, Technical Equipment, Toilets,
Ventilation, Storage

PALOS VERDES (COMPETITION PROPOSAL)
MARCOS CRUZ WITH WANDA YU-YING HU,
GWENOLA KERGALL
PALOS VERDES, 2000

- -
Art Centre

Circulation, Toroidal Structure

MUSEUM OF ART AND TECHNOLOGY
(COMPETITION PROPOSAL)
PRESTON SCOTT COHEN
NEW YORK, 2001

- - - - - - - - - - - - - - - - -
Museum

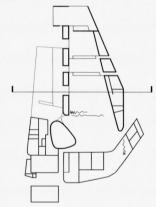

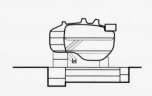

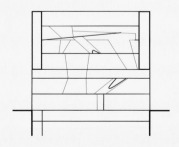

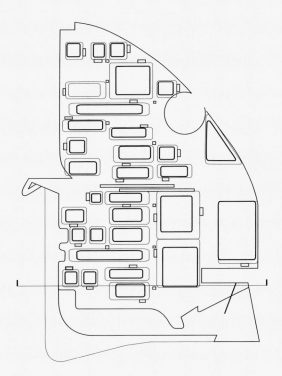

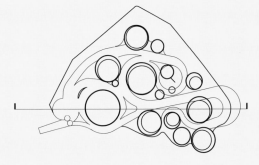

Circulation, Structure, Filtered natural light
through resin membrane, Technical Equipment, Storage, Sitting Facilities, Exhibition
Surface

NEW TOMIHIRO MUSEUM
(COMPETITION PROPOSAL)
MARCOSANDMARJAN
AZUMA VILLAGE, 2002

- - - - - - - - - - - - - - - - -

Museum / Art Centre

Laboratories, Structure, Filtered natural and
artificial light through resin membrane,
Technical Equipment Storage, Circulation,
Office capsules

NEW ENGLAND BIOLABS
(COMPETITION PROPOSAL)
MARCOSANDMARJAN
MASSACHUSETTS, 2001

- -

Laboratories

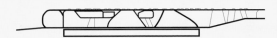

INHABITABLE INTERFACES - COMPARATIVE ANALYSIS

NOTRE-DAME-DU-HAUT
LE CORBUSIER · RONCHAMP, 1950-54

Le Corbusier's chapel of Ronchamp is remarkable for its variety and different interpretations of wall inhabitation. It is an outstanding paradigm of corporeal and physical fleshyness. Ronchamp is characterised by a constant dialogue between both the pilgrims who visit it and the architecture itself. In fact, the whole spatial and physical experience of the chapel works in relation to its walls, enhanced by the surprise of so many spaces and interstices in them. This spatial secrecy has the effect of the architecture revealing itself slowly to us. Orientated towards four cardinal points, each side personalises a different wall character. Walls integrate structure, circulation between outside and inside and filter natural light. They also offer several services such as hosting side chapels, the sacristy and an office in the upper floor (functional wall-inhabitation in the east, north and west façade), along with encasing a statue of Virgin Mary (spiritual wall-inhabitation in the east façade), and also holding the confessionals in its skin (human wall-inhabitation in the west façade), not forgetting the mysterious presence of the 'Modulor' (mathematical wall-inhabitation in all façades).
Although the chapel of Ronchamp might be one of the most illustrated and described buildings of the twentieth century very few reports on the building give attention to the phenomenon of wall inhabitation, in particular, to the intriguing presence of the confessionals. These spaces are small niches that are embedded in the mass of the wall creating a bulge on the outer western façade. But it is interesting to question why Le Corbusier decided to locate these spaces in the wall rather than to iso-

late them as a singular design object, as he would most probably have done in any other of his buildings. Was he just interpreting the tradition of niches and three-dimensional walls of former cathedrals or consciously reinforcing the concept of inhabitable walls in a sacred space? There is nothing that leads to such a conclusion. However, he seems to have understood the confessionals as introspective spaces that would be best placed within the Flesh of Architecture. Consequently, to enter the confessionals one has to creep behind the curtains into the orifices of the wall. The position of the confessionals leaves us facing into the main chapel. However, the low voice of the priest who is behind the inner wooden partition of the confessionals forces us closer to it with our head rotated to the inner side of the wall. Our introspective gaze forces us to look inwards, into the wall, into ourselves. This creates the sensation of being wrapped up in the act of sitting in the wall. In a sense, the wall acquires a quality of maternal enclosure, a spatial womb, as Josep Quetglas would call it.

- -

THE HOUSE OF THE FUTURE
ALISON and PETER SMITHSON
LONDON, 1955-56

The research done by Alison and Peter Smithson in the ninety fifties brings about the emergence of new forms of labour-saving electric appliances, which could be stored away in purpose-built units and simultaneously organise the house in a different manner. Their exhibition installation The House of the Future developed in 1955-56 can be considered the first typological experiment in which the articulation of appliances within scattered Inhabitable Cubicles

create successfully an alternative to traditional corridor/room compartmentalisation of space. Confronted with the emergence of what they called an 'appliance-way-of-life', the increasing number of electronic appliances and different servicing areas are separated into cubicles that emerge from the ground, partly isolated and partly attached to the outer walls. These prefabricated cubicles form a permanent introverted shell structure, which is a turn away from the fluidity of the in-between spaces inside the house.

- -

ASGER JORN MUSEUM
JØRN UTZON · SILKEBORG, 1963

The proposal for the Asger Jorn Museum in Silkeborg, designed by Jørn Utzon in 1963, is a relatively unknown proposal that is the first to make formal and spatial use of a new typological elements that we call Inhabitable Cones. Because of physical limitations of the site, three inhabitable cones of variable size and orientation are placed inside a large hollow space carved into the ground, which is accessible from a curvilinear and sculptural network of ramps and paths. The cones are concealed and enclosed chambers for exhibition purposes, lit from above through a large orifice with natural light and entered from underneath on different levels. In the biggest cone the circulation of one of the ramps is absorbed into the structure snaking around the interstices of its double-layer wall, creating a feeling of physical penetration. The curvature of the path allows the visitor to view the exhibits from slightly different viewpoints. These references refer mainly to the circulation system, in which Utzon allows visitors on the twisting ramp to contemplate the art

INHABITABLE INTERFACES - COMPARATIVE ANALYSIS

works from an enormous difference of angles and heights.

However, the uniqueness and innovation of the proposal for Asger Jorn Museum lies in the combination of circulation and exhibition cones. The cones are three story deep craters, tiled with vivid colours on the outside and painted white in the inside, in which the geometric form and depth of the cones contrasts with the art works being suspended from the ceiling. As Françoise Fromonot[1] explains, Utzon's notion of inhabitation is determined by his understanding of buildings as bodies that have the ability to defend, resist or accept the impositions of the architect. He sees each building as a separate organism, which throughout the complex process of architecture becomes itself a player with its own rules and requirements, in other words, a creature, which we will inhabit. This organic animal-like quality is evident in the fleshy formalisation of the museum.

----

[1] Françoise Fromonot: Jørn Utzon - The Sydney Opera House, Electa architecture 2000 (p. 93)

SAINSBURY CENTRE FOR VISUAL ARTS
NORMAN FOSTER · NORWICH, 1970-74

Norman Foster's Sainsbury Centre for Visual Arts, built in Norwich between 1970 and 1974, is a building that stands out because of the technical and conceptual sophistication of its Inhabitable Walls. With hardly any inner partitions, the building is cleverly reduced to a continuous double-layered structure, which shelters both the inner exhibition spaces and school facilities. While the programme requires very little space division, the inner open space seems to be the result of how the walls are designed. If the building was longer or wider it would hardly change its appearance and functional distribution. Foster's walls are like extruded, horizontal service cores. Roof and walls create a continuum that integrates the structure with the traditional technical services, storage, kitchen, small labs and all sorts of ancillary spaces that require very little space. This exceptional and 'clean' typological concept, which is determined by the rhythm of the structure and the outer panelling, emerges from a late decision of 'thickening' the walls, freeing the area in-between to an ultimately open and flexible space. This building is its walls and the resulting inner space.

CENTRE GEORGE POMPIDOU
RICHARD ROGERS/RENZO PIANO
PARIS, 1971-77

The Centre George Pompidou was a competition won by Richard Rogers and Renzo Piano in July 1971, and was built in Paris between 1972 and 1977. It reflects more than any other building of its time the ideas of Cedric Price for his Fun Palace project, 1962, and Archigram's visions (for example, Mike Webb's Sin Centre, 1959-62). Simultaneously presenting itself as a entertainment and culture park with gigantic electronic billboards on which the cultural programme of its inner spaces are displayed to the city and open to the general public. The main façade that provides access at all levels acts as a giant public notice board, which reflects the pop-culture of its time. As in the Sainsbury Centre for Visual Arts, the typological strength of both buildings lies in the programmatic and conceptual intensity of the wall-façades, i.e. avoiding wall divisions in flexible, functional and transparent inner spaces.

But the importance of the Pompidou Centre lies in the relationship between the building and the city itself, created by the inhabited façade that prompts a continuum between inside and outside. The façade defines its inhabited surface as a space from which the transient inhabitant both sees and is being seen. The inhabited façade of the piazza exposes the main circulation as a type of hymn for a mobile society, whose inhabitants can be interpreted as a combination between Kisho Kurokawa's concept of a 'Homo-movens' - a highly mobile figure that emerges in Japanese Metabolism - and Cedric Price's 'Homo-stimulus' - a character from the British post-war era.

KUNSTHAAL
REM KOOLHAAS / OMA · ROTTERDAM, 1988-92

Another art centre that hosts large internal exhibition spaces is Rem Koolhas' / OMA's Kunsthaal, built in Rotterdam between 1988 and 1992. It is different from the previous projects, insofar as it is internally compartmentalised and structured through the arrangement of its inner areas rather than an outer inhabitable façade. The concept of the exhibition spaces is a continuous inner circuit through various exhibition spaces, crossed by two external routes that are perpendicular to each other: a north-south pedestrian ramp that links the lower public garden with the upper main boulevard, and a east-west road that runs parallel to the Massboulevard allowing access for vehicles to the lower exhibition floor. This complex circulation scheme divides the building into four parts locating the main access for the building right at its centre. The Inhabitable Wall that is placed along

INHABITABLE INTERFACES - COMPARATIVE ANALYSIS

the pedestrian route is thus at the centre of the circulation, both existing as an outside façade and an inner wall. Human encounter with the wall varies conceptually. It hosts in its interstices the ancillary storage rooms, along with the service lifts, toilets of the cafeteria, ventilation shafts, and both the entrances to the cafeteria in the lower ground and the exhibition spaces in the upper levels. In the latter we find the ticket office where people sell tickets from within the wall inside. Then one walks along the wall inside the auditorium, downwards or upwards crossing it to enter the other side of the exhibition spaces. At a certain point the wall pokes out of the roof as a tower for advertisements. But apart from its volumetric presence it is also the transparent materiality of the corrugated fibreglass and the punctuated appearance of neon lights in its interior that characterises the wall as a light-wall. Koolhaas' wall is the cheapest part of the building yet operates as its centrepiece.

- - - - - - - - - - - - - - - - - - - -

SEDAI MEDIATHEQUE
TOYO ITO • SENDAI, 1997-01

A forest of Inhabitable Columns scattered randomly throughout five juxtaposed floor plates characterises Toyo Ito's Mediatheque in Sendai developed between 1997 and 2001. The columns are functionally service cores, containing staircases, elevators and ventilation ducts, which have however a strong conceptual richness. They are simultaneously vertical conduits of people, information and energies such as light air and water. Their planimetric layout conveys movement and introduces a spatial scattering that enhances the fluidity of the space. This is especially clear by the fact that none of the tubes

touch the floor or ceiling directly, giving an impression of a flowing-through system.

Ito's view of the world we inhabit is defined by flows rather than by static structures. Apart from the traditional vertical flow of air and water, invisible flows of electrons pass through the tubes, along with digital data that has become present with the use of computers. But the scattered organisation of the tubes also produces an impression of swirling motion throughout each floor plain, defining the physical movement of the visitors as "gliding or even swimming as if one were a fish in an aquarium"[2].

- - - - - - - - - - - - - - - - - - - -

[2] Antoine Picon, Anna Agoston: Building in the Information Age: On Architectural Meaning and its Limits in Ron Witte: Case: Toyo Ito - Sendai Mediatheque, Harvard University graduate School of Design, Prestel Verlag 2002 (p. 62)

- - - - - - - - - - - - - - - - - - - -

KUNSTHAUS GRAZ
PETER COOK and COLIN FOURNIER
GRAZ, 2000-03

A team lead by Peter Cook and Colin Fournier takes the idea of a continuous skin to its extreme in the competition project for the Kunsthaus in Graz developed in 2000. The building is lifted up off the ground and every function, apart from the exhibition spaces, is literally embedded into a completely autonomous inhabitable building wall, highlighted by several wall-incorporated audio-devices and stretchable media-cells. There is an underpinning belief that the architectural skin itself can trigger a varied and rich spatial experience. To discover the Kunsthaus is to feel an intense relationship between a body in movement and the building's skin. The skin is pierced from the outside, via the escalator,

which acts as a 'pin' that emerges from underneath the 'belly', into the first floor inside. The experience of the escalator piercing the inside of the building is highly dramatic. One ascends into the unknown, zigzagging from one corner of one floor to the other of the next floor of the building until reaching the spectacular upper floor. From here one then rediscovers the city by stepping out onto the upper bar, called the 'needle'.

It is also possible to peep through the lowest light nozzle out at the old Cuckoo tower of the castle in Graz.

In the competition stage the initial ideas for the skin were based on bio-technological phenomena. It was thought as a flexible membrane that could make the nozzles grow and rotate always against the orientation of the sun, and therefore control the incision of natural light on the interior upper spaces. The skin was also proposed as an 'inlucent' surface variable in its degrees of opacity/transparency. The embedded technological apparatus, along with internal activity could therefore shimmer through to the outside and create an effect of intrigue on the front façade. Some parts of the building's skin could even be replaced and dressed differently according to the changing inner programme.

- - - - - - - - - - - - - - - - - - - -

MUSEUM OF ART AND TECHNOLOGY
PRESTON SCOTT COHEN • NEW YORK, 2001

The competition project for the Museum of Art and Technology in New York, proposed by Preston Scott Cohen in 2001, presents an innovative typology of a variety of Inhabitable Circulation Tubes. There function is mainly for circulation purposes, since the other ancillary functions, such as toilets and fire

INHABITABLE INTERFACES - COMPARATIVE ANALYSIS

staircases are integrated into two serv-
ice-walls on both side of the building.
But the intersection of the so-called
'toroidal' structure and the apparently
random location of diagonal circulation
tubes create a surprising and changing spatial arrangement on each floor.
The visitor is a kind of contemporary
'flanêur' who circulates through opaque
tubes being repeatedly submerged into
the unknown and popping-up somewhere
where the architectural landscape can't
be recognised. This sensation of spatial
disorientation and simultaneous discovery of the unknown is strengthened by
the connection of floors with each other
that are not contiguous, such as the
ground-floor with the second, fourth and
sixth floors when ascending, and the
seventh, fifth, third and first floor when
descending to the main entrance.

- -

PALOS VERDES ART CENTRE
MARCOS CRUZ with YU-YING HU
and GWENOLA KERGALL
LOS ANGELES, 2000

The idea of a one-story high building
with a double Inhabitable Wall reap-
pears in the project for the Palos Verdes Art Centre, which is a Los Angeles
competition proposal done in 2000.
The wall and ceiling, as in Foster's
Sainsbury Centre for Visual Arts create a
continuum in which several services and
interactive devices are incorporated.
The inclination of the natural landscape
prompted an architectural landscape:
the building takes over the slope in a
sequence of ascending exhibition spaces, which culminate in a main patio.
A metal tensegrity skeleton that holds
in place an extended cocoon of silicon
around the gallery spaces defines the
building structure. The silicon is lightly
tinted and filters light through its 'en-
lucent' materiality. This also affords
an even and soft light to its enclosed
spaces. Photo-chromatic chemicals
embedded within the silicon allow an
automatic control of heat and humidity
levels. A multitude of individual entities personify the real inhabitants of
the building, acting as ventilation hairs
that colonise the roof. These 'ventilation hairs' draw air through the space in
a venturi effect. As the wind blows the
hairs are gently bent animating the art
centre. The silicon skin plays host to a
variety of interactive devices that para-
sitically inhabit its malleable surface.
Ventilation hairs, sensing visitor movement, trigger a cam that causes the
hairs to twitch or gesture at passers-by.
Furthermore the natural 'give' of the
silicon material registers any type of
movement including earth movements
be they by a truck or earth-tremor
which are translated into architectural
movements.

- -

NEW ENGLAND BIOLABS
MARCOSANDMARJAN
MASSACHUSETTS, 2001
(see pages 74-77)

- -

NEW TOMIHIRO MUSEUM
MARCOSANDMARJAN
AZUMA VILLAGE, 2002
(See pages 78 - 83)

Lofting House

Proposal for a house in Moita, for the exhibition A Casa
Portuguesa – Mudando a Arte
de Habitar at the ExperimentaDesign, Lisbon Portugal, 2005

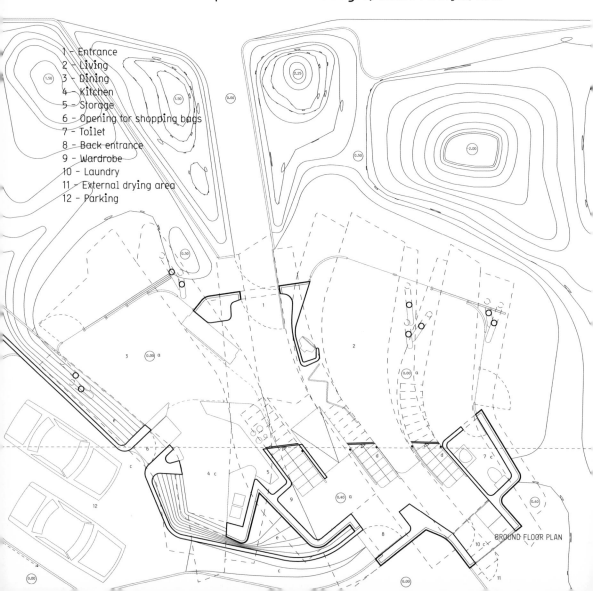

1 – Entrance
2 – Living
3 – Dining
4 – Kitchen
5 – Storage
6 – Opening for shopping bags
7 – Toilet
8 – Back entrance
9 – Wardrobe
10 – Laundry
11 – External drying area
12 – Parking

GROUND FLOOR PLAN

13 – room 1
14 – toilet area
15 – stairs to room 1 and library
16 – library
17 – room 2
18 – toilet area
19 – stairs to room 2
20 – room 3
21 – toilet area
22 – stairs to room 3

corte transversal

FIRST FLOOR PLAN

Client » L'Atalante, with ExperimentaDesign and Corte-Real
Organisers » Carlos Sant'Ana, Pedro Machado Costa
Team » Design: marcosandmarjan › Collaboration: Tze-Chun Wei,
Wanda Yu-Ying Hu

- -

The house is part of an experimental (housing) project where 12 architects were invited to propose contemporary concepts of dwelling. For this purpose a site was chosen in the suburban area of Moita, south of Lisbon.

For the Lofting House a simple division of programme is proposed - the public spaces are spread out on the ground floor, while the private spaces hover above in a series of vessels.

Private spaces are understood as autonomous territories within the house with independent use, access and views. These areas are rather like individual apartments that can be connected or separated from each other. Family members or people not from the same family aggregate can cohabit within the house. The spatial configuration of the rooms is determined by a sequence of structural Inhabitable Walls, creating loft spaces that are organised in longitudinal volumes with east-west orientation. The multiplicity of domestic functions, such as sleeping, cleaning, working or communicating is transferred from the traditional room-space into wall-interfaces. Consequently, the notion of bedroom, working space, toilet or bathroom closet is abolished and the appliances disseminated within the walls.

The public areas are treated in a rather flexible manner waiting to be organised and furnished by the future occupants of the house. Since the lifestyle of inhabitants in such a house does not follow preconceived domestic routines or taste standards (which was common in the traditional bourgeois family), the arrangement and use of the public domains is left open and treated as rather undefined areas. However, there is an atmospheric intensity felt through the interpenetration of artificial and natural landscapes. The large surface of laser-cut window screens and louver-like panels create an ornamented dress around the public spaces that filter light, air and the view over the garden. When the façade is open-up, the boundary between interior and exterior space becomes blurred and the public realm is enlarged to the perimeter of the garden.

There are two proposed entrances: a west-side more formal entrance that can be used by visitors and people who walk into the house, and an east-side entrance that serves the daily needs of the inhabitants who arrive by car.

The garage acquires an import role, both as the most commonly used entrance of the house, as well as a sort of horizontal wall that protects the house from its surrounding. From here the inhabitants can deliver shopping bags through a wall orifice directly into the kitchen, before accessing the house through a double-height lobby with a direct link to the upper rooms.

VIEW OF ROOF

Feira Internacional dos Açores

Proposal for the Azores International Fair,
for the exhibition L'Atalante at the Academia das Artes
dos Açores, Ponta Delgada Portugal, 2005 [31.06.05-31.08.05]

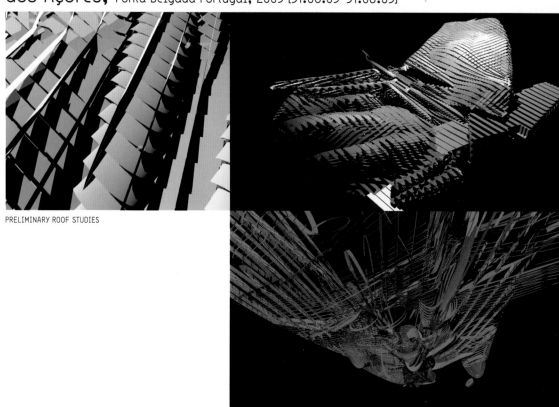

PRELIMINARY ROOF STUDIES

STUDIES OF ORNAMENTAL TRUSSES

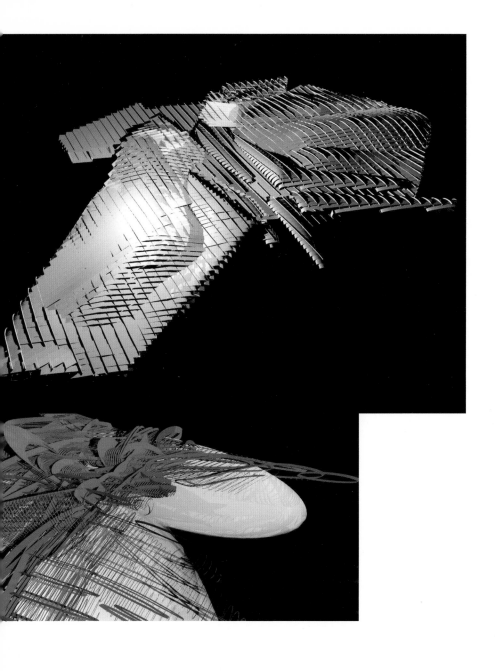

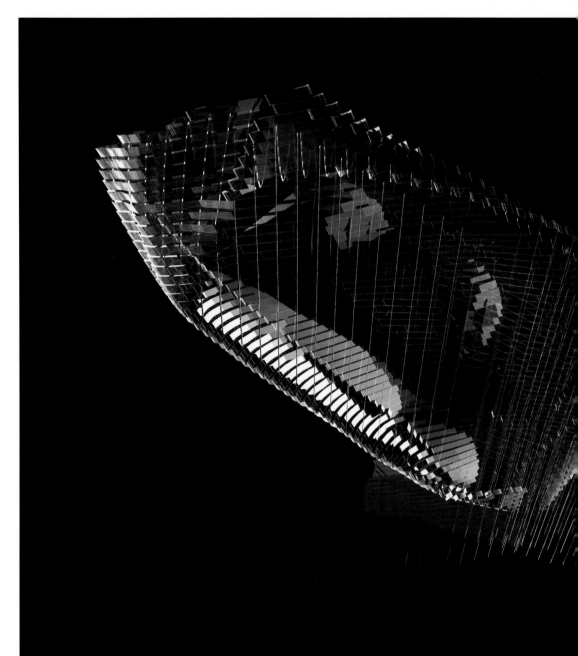

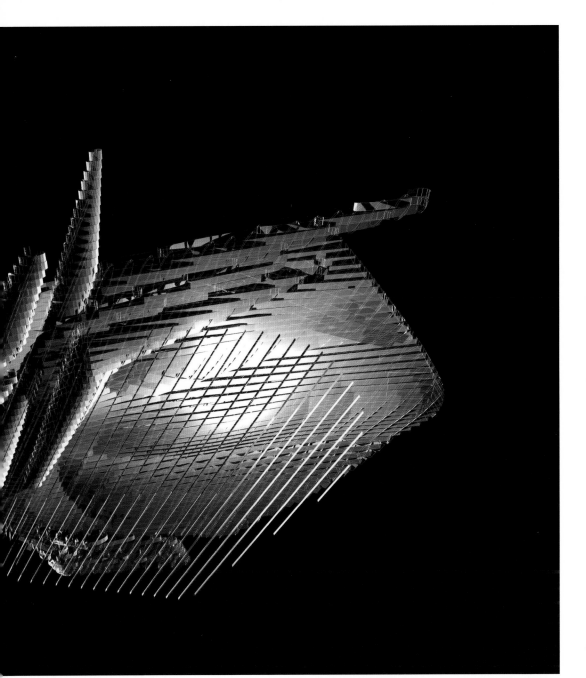

VIEW FROM UNDERNEATH OF ROOF CONSTRUCTION WITH EMBEDDED OFFICES

SECTIONING OF ROOF STRUCTURE

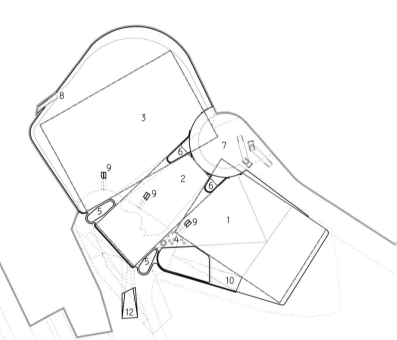

1. Exhibition hall 1
2. Exhibition hall 2
3. Exhibition hall 3
4. Cafe stand
5. Lifts, toilets and service areas
6. Storage
7. Shipping area
8. Emergency Staircase
9. Escalator to main entrance
10. Main access ramp
11. Exterior Exhibition areas
12. External public ramp to main entrance

BASEMENT PLAN

GENERAL VIEW FROM ABOVE

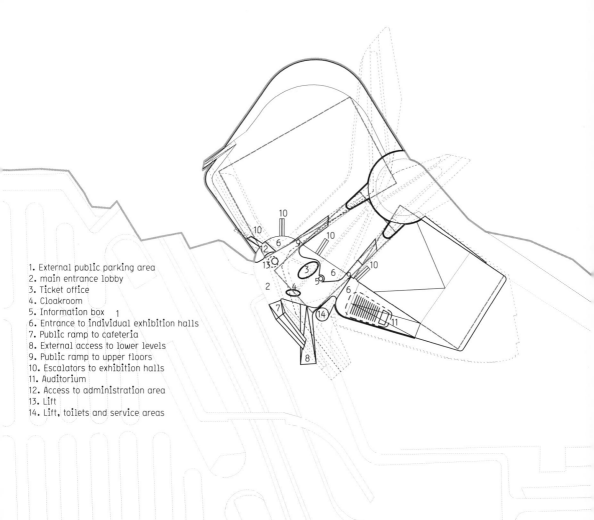

1. External public parking area
2. main entrance lobby
3. Ticket office
4. Cloakroom
5. Information box
6. Entrance to individual exhibition halls
7. Public ramp to cafeteria
8. External access to lower levels
9. Public ramp to upper floors
10. Escalators to exhibition halls
11. Auditorium
12. Access to administration area
13. Lift
14. Lift, toilets and service areas

GROUND FLOOR PLAN

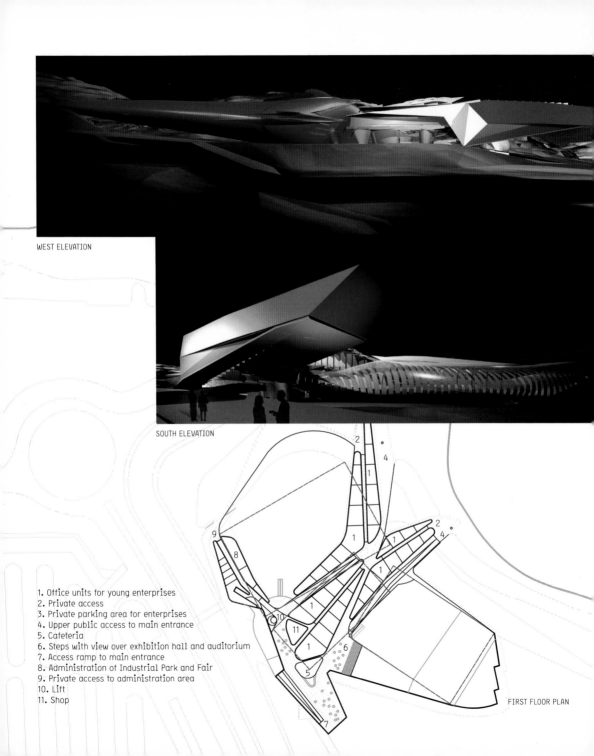

WEST ELEVATION

SOUTH ELEVATION

1. Office units for young enterprises
2. Private access
3. Private parking area for enterprises
4. Upper public access to main entrance
5. Cafeteria
6. Steps with view over exhibition hall and auditorium
7. Access ramp to main entrance
8. Administration of Industrial Park and Fair
9. Private access to administration area
10. Lift
11. Shop

FIRST FLOOR PLAN

INTERNAL VIEW OF EXHIBITION HALLS

AERIAL VIEW FROM NORTH

Team » Design: marcosandmarjan › Collaborators: João Albuquerque, Marco Sacchi, Shui Liu

Programme/Areas » Exhibition halls / food and beverage: 7995 m² › Shipping areas / storage: 1498 m² › Administration / spaces for new enterprises: 2755 m² › External circulation area: 2530 m² › External exhibition area: 8350 m²

- -

Programme » The Azores International Fair belongs to the Ponta Delgada Industrial Park on the Azores Islands, hosting a variety of programmes that can be used 24h a day. It is proposed to incorporate three large exhibition halls for small and medium-size fairs with a vast external exhibition surface, food and beverage areas and spaces for new enterprises, as well as the administration of the whole Industrial Park.

Concept » The programme is internally organised as the result of a spatial dialectic relationship between the mass of the existing topography and the floating roof of the building. While the building in the north side is excavated in order to create various exhibition craters, the rest of the programme is embedded in the inhabitable trusses of the roof, which is lifted up from the ground through a complex system of structural walls, ramps and escalators.

Circulation » A circulation network open to the public connects the fair with its context in three distinct levels thus crossing the building. On the east side, at the highest point of the site, is located the access to the spaces for new enterprises with a private parking area. On the west side, at the intermediate level, is located the main entrance within the roof structure, allowing direct access from the large public parking areas in front of the building, and access to the restaurants and cafeterias inside. This floor creates a mezzanine floor from where one can visualize the whole infrastructure before submerging into the exhibition halls on the lower floor. Here are located three large halls in a sequence that can be used simultaneously as closed spaces with independent accesses, or as one large exhibition space, which can be extended to the exterior through the south façade.

Site integration » The building is proposed as a self-contained, yet permeable system in terms of its circulation and relationship with its context, as well as in the form in which it materialises its largely glased elevations. These are partially ornamented with sophisticated control mechanisms for illumination and ventilation purposes.

The specific climatic and topographic conditions of the Azores Islands suggest a reflection of natural elements on the tectonic definition of the building, not only in terms of technology, but also in symbolic terms: The presence of the earth appears in form of the exhibition craters, while the phenomenon of water is reinterpreted in the fluidity of the circulation; the notion of fire is expressed in the ornamented design of the roof structure, while the air (wind) is felt in the floating presence of the roof and through the considerable cantilever of the cafeteria, which is projected over the surrounding landscape.

Bai Jia Zhuang

Proposal for an office and retail complex, Beijing P. R. China, 2004

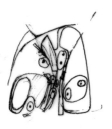
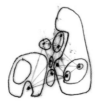
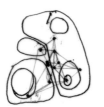

PRELIMINARY SKETCHES OF PLANS

Ground 0

+ 10 m

+ 20 m

+ 30

EAST ELEVATION ALONG THE THIRD RING ROAD

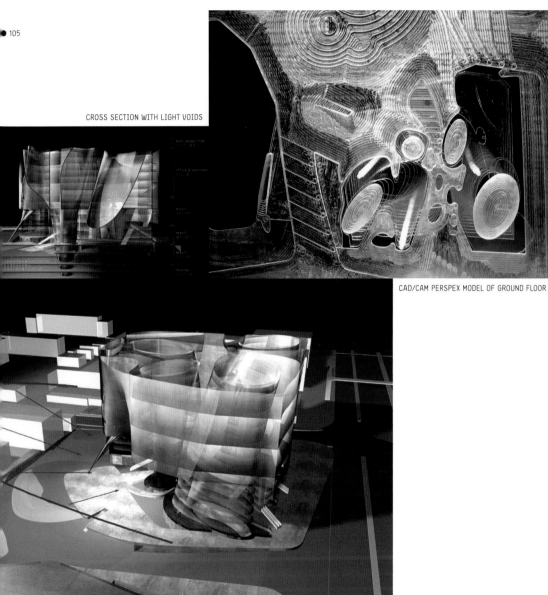

CROSS SECTION WITH LIGHT VOIDS

CAD/CAM PERSPEX MODEL OF GROUND FLOOR

SOUTH VIEW

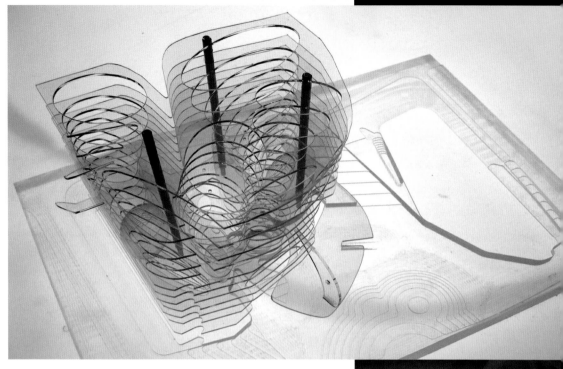

PLAN WITH JUXTAPOSED LEVELS

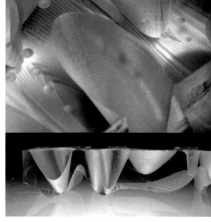

PRELIMINARY PERSPEX MODEL OF VOIDS

Team » Design: marcosandmarjan with Jia Lu and Steve Pike
Programme » Offices Retail: 26860m² › Apartments: 33320m² › Sports and enter-
tainment areas: 2550m² › Parking: 23600m² › External Green Areas: 3700m²
Total construction area: 90.000m²

- -

The building is sited on the eastern side of the busy Third Ring Road in Beijing.
Positioned at the leading public edge of the site, the building allows for the
creation of a public garden at the back, from where the main access to the
retail spaces can occur. By reinforcing the edges of the urban block, the building is presented with a clear urban façade, whilst maximising visually exposed
elevations for advertising opportunities. Prime locations for acoustic protection
are established by this approach, enhancing the quality of the internal spaces.
The vertical organisation of the proposal is deliberately simple. The basement hosts vehicle parking, plant rooms and additional ancillary activities.
The ground level merges the upper subterranean level and the lower above
ground level into a common public zone reserved for retail activities, while the
remaining levels above are dedicated to residential/commercial (office) use.
At roof level, there is the opportunity to provide a unique, high quality public
space of terraces and restaurants.
At the lower public levels the mass of the building dissipates amongst a cluster
of volumes, supporting structures, routes, and level variations. In this region,
the proposal knits into the surrounding urban fabric, providing a circulation filter. The pace of movement is slowed, the intimacy is heightened and the retail
interface is maximised.
In order to provide optimum access to light, the proposal locates the open public space to the brighter region of the site, evading the predominantly shaded
areas resulting from the constructed building volumes. A series of light wells,
perforating the mass of the building, allow for the majority of internal spaces
to have access to daylight, further increasing the quality of the residential/
commercial levels. The presence of these puncturing voids has the additional
benefit of varying the spatial experience of the proposal.
Despite the apparent complexity, the principles of the construction are those
of a standard layered load bearing assembly. A certain economy of structure is
employed, in that a number of vertical supports have the dual function of bearing floor loads and framing the intruding light wells. The attitude of producing
a series of clustered elements and volumes, rather than an object with defini-
tive boundaries, supports future potential expansion of the site and proposal.

CAD/CAM AND LASER-CUT MODEL

Xiyuan Entertainment Complex

Preliminary project stages for an entertainment complex,

Beijing, P. R. China, 2004

CAD/CAM MODEL OF INITIAL ROOF STUDIES

AERIAL VIEW WITH MAIN ENTRANCE TO SUMMER PALACE ON NORTHWEST
SIDE, LAKE, AND PROPOSAL OF XIYUAN ENTERTAINMENT COMPLEX

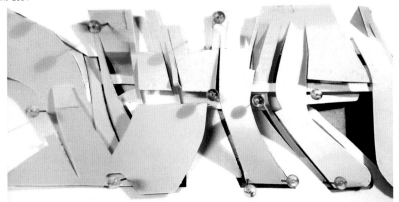

CARDBOARD MODEL WITH
PERPENDICULAR ARRANGEMENT
OF BUILDINGS

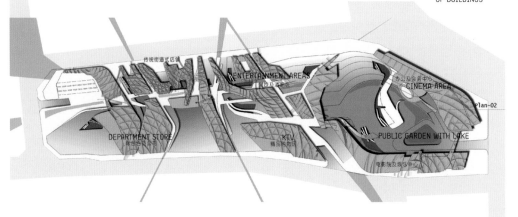

GROUND FLOOR PLAN

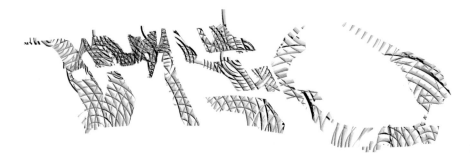

ROOF PLAN

Client » Beijing Xinjing Yihe Real Estate Development Ltd
Team » Design: marcosandmarjan with Jia Lu, Competition stage: with Jia Lu
and Steve Pike › Collaborators: Nat Keast, Shaun Siu Chong, James Pike, Sirichai Bunchua) › Renderings: Mark Exon, Samuel White, Kenny Tsui, Tamsin Green,
Jessica Lee) › Model: Sirichai Bunchua, Keith Watson, Andy Shawn Engineering, Beijing Design Institute › Total Built Area: 180.000 m² › Ground floor area:
56.000 m² › Basement area on -6 level: 56.000 m² › Basement on -9.6 level:
50.000 m² (car park) + 6.000 m² (units) › Road and external circulation: 12.000
m² › Estimated Construction Cost: 526.000.000 Renminbi (approx. €51.538.430)

- -

The Xiyuan Entertainment Complex is located in front of the gates to the Yiheyu-
an Royal Summer Palace in the Haidian district in northwest Beijing, China. The
proximity to the Royal Palace constrains the design of the commercial intervention towards a low-rise building typology, conceived as a three-dimensional
garden landscape capped by a fragmented yet smooth roof surface of stone and
green areas, simultaneously permeable to light and sight. The journey through
the boundary of the intervention is transitional. The visitor arrives at the more
introspective spaces of the site; pace slows down and the relationship with
the intervention is concentrated. Retail and entertainment are encouraged in
a sequence of protected courtyards, gardens, footpaths and streets organized
perpendicularly to the North Boulevard and the South thoroughfare. Intimate,
narrow paths and dramatic, spacious malls interconnect. A lattice of ramps and
sweeping roofs overlap and occasionally merge in an exchange between buildings, hard landscape and green spaces.

The program of the Xiyuan Entertainment Complex is divided into two Major Entertainment Groups and eight Commercial Unit Buildings. The first group of Major Entertainment Groups include eight Cinemas, a KTV, Indoor Games, and an
Exhibition Area. These facilities are located on the busier east side of the site
close to the Underground station and the urban thoroughfare. They are grouped
together into one building complex with a major distribution area (foyer) that
simultaneously connects the upper ground floor entrances, proposed road and
underground station on the -6 level. The exhibition area is located strategi-
cally between the North Boulevard and the main urban thoroughfare, whereas
the KTV is placed on the most visible eastern corner of the side. The cluster of
three hotel units is located on the calmer west side surrounded by a wall that
safeguards and protects the peacefulness of the interiors.

The Commercial Unit are distributed in eight separate buildings. The sequence
of these autonomously standing volumes organises the underneath common car
park and also the use of the upper roof areas. It also allows for a separate
management of units, as well as a possible phasing during the construction
time. The spaces between the Unit Buildings create a sequence of interstices
through which outer and/or inner circulation between buildings and plazas on
different levels is established. These interstices are designed to be circulation
spaces that enable direct ventilation and insulation for the majority of units.

FOAMBOARD MODEL

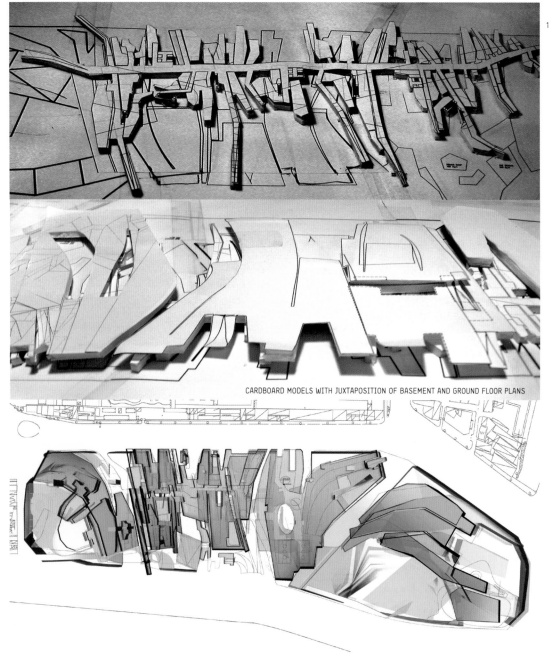

CARDBOARD MODELS WITH JUXTAPOSITION OF BASEMENT AND GROUND FLOOR PLANS

A 500m long and 16 m wide road strip - the Xiyuan Avenue - through the middle of the site intersects each Unit Building, dividing it into a northern and a southern sector. The northern section is smaller and more appropriate to the pedestrian flow of tourists along the North Boulevard. The bigger southern sector contains larger inner units that relate more to the quicker pace of the high intensity car flow. From the Xiyuan Avenue, the grouping of all units into Unit Buildings enhances the intervention's urban character, in particular through the variety of façades and in-between open spaces. From the south and north Boulevards, on the other hand, the gaps between buildings interweave gradually the landscape with the proposed built form, minimising the impact in such delicate site.

All individual Units inside the Unit Buildings are divided into duplex typologies with direct car access on the front façade (either from the South thoroughfare or the Xiyuan Avenue). In many cases there is also a pedestrian access provided on the floor underneath or above the duplex unit (either from the North Boulevard or the ground floor path along the Xiyuan Avenue, called Xiyuan Promenade). Internal Circulation Nodes within the duplex units integrate staircases, escalators, toilets and/or small office spaces in an in-between mezzanine floor. Crossing staircases of two neighbouring units allow for a visual interchange between users of different units.

In order to achieve the percentage of green area required by the Beijing Municipality (30% of ground floor area), all buildings and roads where grouped into a dense cluster of buildings in the middle of the site, creating a green belt all around it. On the south side, the green area is larger than on the north side and is occupied with a barrier of dense and tall vegetation that shields the view towards the extensive wall along the South thoroughfare. This longitudinal urban park integrates external parking, pavements, recreation spots and several water pools. On the north Boulevard, the belt is kept narrow in order to allow a close contact between tourists that walk along the Boulevard and the facing building façades. The western part of the belt is proposed as a ramping surface for luxurious vegetation that surrounds the hotel volume touching the lower floors of the hotels. The ramping surface of the green area brings natural light and ventilation to the dining rooms and reception of each hotel in the -6 level.

There are three types of proposed plazas in the Xiyuan Entertainment Complex: two Sunken Plazas in the car park - The West Sunken Plaza and the East Sunken Plaza - a larger plaza on the -6 level - the Xiyuan Piazza - and several courtyards in the ground floor level of each building - the Upper Courtyards.

The Sunken plazas are small longitudinal spaces surrounded by unit are covered with glass roofs that allow natural light to reach the lower levels of the project. These areas enhance the spatial quality of the project by extending the programme into an area, the car park, that otherwise would remain as rather tedious and unattractive space. The Xiyuan Piazza is an open space that results from the extension of the larger green area into the middle of the site and the Xiyuan Avenue. It is a space surrounded by cafeterias and restaurants

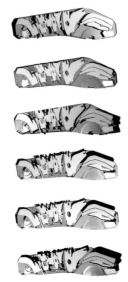

STUDY OF SUN INSULATION

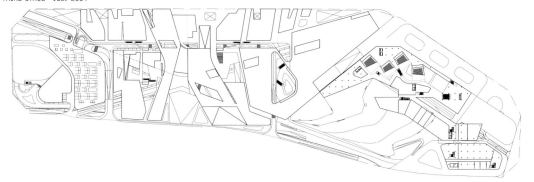

ROOF PLAN

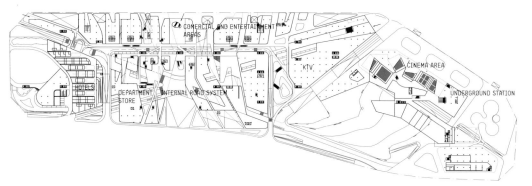

COMERCIAL AND ENTERTAINMENT AREAS

KTV

CINEMA AREA

UNDERGROUND STATION

HOTELS

DEPARTMENT STORE

INTERNAL ROAD SYSTEM

FIRST BASEMENT FLOOR

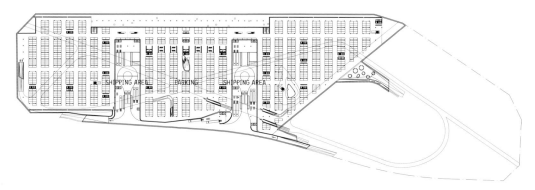

SHIPPING AREA

PARKING

SHIPPING AREA

SECOND BASEMENT PLAN

CARDBOARD MODEL WITH INTERNAL ROAD SYSTEM

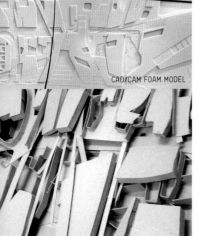

CAD/CAM FOAM MODEL

TWO-AND-A-HALF DIMENSIONALITY OF ROOF

and where water recreation activities can take place. The Upper Courtyards are conceptually rooted in traditional high status Chinese buildings. They are small enclosed areas in the Commercial Units which vary in form and shape according to the anatomy of each individual building. As backyard spaces that can be open or enclosed they are both private and public, establishing a link between the backside of different units. These spaces are connected via External Circulation Nodes located on the edge of the buildings with the roof and the underneath car park.

The vertical organisation of the whole intervention follows the required proposition of three juxtaposed layers: the sunken ground floor at -1meters, the basement level at -6 meters and the car park level at -9.6 meters. All buildings guarantee a maximum of 3.3m eve height along the whole site with the exception of the eastern cinema and KTV volume that grows to 6.6m from the ground. This height is important to create a more urban scale along the busy eastern thoroughfare, simultaneously announcing the flat presence of the whole entertainment complex.

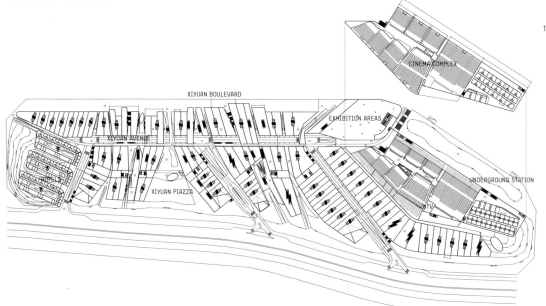

GROUND FLOOR PLAN WITH CINEMA AND
EXHIBITION AREAS, ENTERTAINMENT
UNITS, AND THREE HOTELS

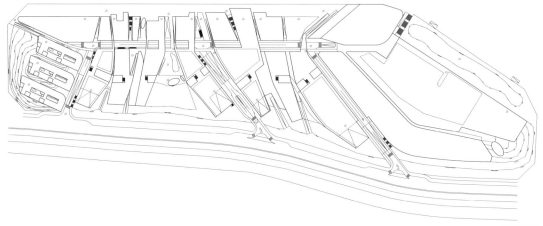

ROOF PLAN

GENERAL VIEW FROM SOUTH WITH XIYUAN PIAZZA

VIEW OF XIYUAN AVENUE WITH URBAN FAÇADES

CARDBOARD MODEL

The external materiality of the Xiyuan Entertainment Complex follows the examples of great Chinese architecture. Whilst the structural skeleton is proposed out of reinforced concrete, stone originally from the the Beijing area is proposed as the main cladding material, defining the external appearance of façades and roofs. Metal and glass will be used on the large exposed unit façades to the North Boulevard and Xiyuan Avenue, and will exceptionally be exposed on the volume of the cinemas and KTV to eastern side.

HORIZONTAL SECTIONS OF SKIN

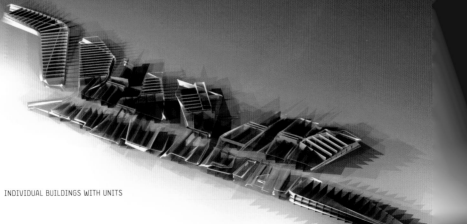

INDIVIDUAL BUILDINGS WITH UNITS

GENERAL VIEW FROM NORTH
SIDE WITH PEDESTRIAN ROUTE
ALONG XIYUAN BOULEVARD

ACKNOWLEDGEMENTS

THANKS TO PATRICK EHRHARDT AND WOLFGANG FIEL FOR INVITING US
TO PARTICIPATE IN THE HAMBURG EXHIBITION AND THEIR SUPPORT TO MAKE THIS
BOOK POSSIBLE. WE ARE GRATEFUL TO PROF. JONATHAN HILL AND DORIS FRITZ
FOR THEIR COMMENTS DURING THE DEVELOPMENT OF THE PUBLICATION, AND IN
PARTICULAR APPRECIATIVE TO ANTÓNIO SILVEIRA GOMES AND MAFALDA ANJOS
FOR THEIR TREMENDOUS EFFORT IN DESIGNING THIS BOOK IN SUCH SHORT TIME.

SPECIAL THANKS TO PROF. SIMON CHU AND DR. BEATRICE PEINI GYSEN-HSIEH
FOR THEIR SUPPORT DURING THE FENG CHIA & BARTLETT DIGITAL ARCHITECTURE
WORKSHOP IN TAICHUNG TAIWAN AND THE PRODUCTION OF THE SPLINEWALL.
WE ARE PARTICULARLY THANKFUL TO DR. BEATRICE PEINI GYSEN-HSIEH,
LEE PING-HSUN, TEO BOON TING AND PO CHUAN CHEN FOR THEIR HELP IN
SETTING-UP THE SPLINEWALL AT THE CONSEQUENCE HAMBURG EXHIBITION.

THE PROJECTS PRESENTED HERE WOULD NOT BE POSSIBLE WITHOUT THE HELP OF
ALL WHO COLLABORATED WITH US DURING THESE YEARS. THIS INCLUDES ANDRÉS
AGUILAR, ANDY SHAW, HUI HUI TEOH, JAMES PIKE, JENS RITTER, JESSICA LEE, JIA
LU, JOÃO ALBUQUERQUE, KEITH WATSON, KENNY TSUI, TAMSIN GREEN, LIU SHUI,
MARCO SACCHI, MARK EXON, NAT KEAST, PO CHUAN CHEN, SAMUEL WHITE, SIRICHAI
BUNCHUA, SHAO MING, SHAUN SIU-CHONG, STEVE PIKE, TOBIAS KLEIN, TSE-JUN
WEI, WANDA YU-YING HU, STUDENTS OF UNIT 20 IN 2003-2004, STUDENTS AT
THE DIGITAL ARCHITECTURE WORKSHOP TAIWAN 2005, AS WELL AS ASSOCIATE
ARCHITECTS MARI VIINIKAINEN AND ANTONIO GUEDES.

WE TAKE THE OPPORTUNITY TO THANK PEDRO ALBUQUERQUE AT THE CML IN LISBON
FOR HIS UNCONDITIONAL SUPPORT DURING THE WHOLE PROCESS OF THE 75ª FEIRA
DO LIVRO DE LISBOA, AS WELL AS ARTUR NEVES OF CONTUBOS FOR HIS ADVICES
AND HELP DURING THE CONSTRUCTION OF THE CAFETERIA/AUDITORIUM BUILDING.

AFTER ALL, WE ARE INDEBTED TO PROF. PETER COOK FOR HIS ENDLESS ENTHUSIASM
AND BELIEVE IN ARCHITECTURE AND THE UNCONDITIONAL SUPPORT FOR OUR
CAREERS SINCE WE ARRIVED IN LONDON IN 1998.

OUR GRATITUDE IS ENDLESS FOR THE HELP AND PATIENCE OF WANDA YU-YING HU
AND UTE PERNTHALER DURING ALL THESE YEARS OF INTENSIVE WORK.

PHOTOGRAPHY CREDITS
ALEJANDRO ROMANUTTI (P. 71), MARKUS FREISINGER (P.60), STEVE PIKE (P.106,
107, 111), VIRGILIO FERREIRA (P. 52-55), TSE-JUN WEI (P.20,21), WANDA YU-YING
HU (P. 46, 79), MARCOS CRUZ AND MARJAN COLLETTI (REST).

ILLUSTRATION CREDITS
MIKE WEBB (P. 68-69)

DESIGN BY BARBARA SAYS...